on track ...
The Kinks

every album, every song

Martin Hutchinson

sonicbondpublishing.com

Sonicbond Publishing Limited
www.sonicbondpublishing.co.uk
Email: info@sonicbondpublishing.co.uk

First Published in the United Kingdom 2022
First Published in the United States 2022

British Library Cataloguing in Publication Data:
A Catalogue record for this book is available from the British Library

ISBN 978-1-78952-172-6

Typeset in ITC Garamond & ITC Avant Garde
Printed and bound in England

Graphic design and typesetting: Full Moon Media

Acknowledgements

There are many people I'd like to thank for help, advice, information and encouragement. So, in no particular order, many thanks to the following: Stephen Lambe at Sonicbond Publishing for having faith, Stasi Roe @ MBCPR, Geoff Lewis and Olga Ruocco at the Kinksfan Kollectiv, Dave Emlen @ KindaKinks.net for information and images, Steve Meekings at X Records in Bolton, and John Dalton, Dave Clarke, Rick Wakeman, and Steve Harley for their contributions.

Also, to my wife Michaela and daughter Emma, for their love and encouragement. And of course my little ginger tom-cat Sydney. Thank you all!

In loving memory of Darwin, my beloved cat (2015 – 2021), who spent much of the time I spent writing this book on my lap.

on track ...

The Kinks

Contents

Introduction and Notes

I have always been aware of the music of The Kinks. When 'You Really Got Me' got to the top of the UK singles chart, I had just turned five years old. My elder sister was a teenager and was always listening to Radio Luxembourg and Radio Caroline in the evenings, and of course, *Top Of The Pops* was required viewing on Thursday nights. However, it was to be over a decade later – in 1976 – when I really got into them. It was the Pye Records *Golden Hour* Kinks compilation album that did it, and I devoured the music. I bought my first new Kinks album in 1978. It was *Misfits*, and today – 40 years on – it's still my favourite Kinks album.

Over the years, I have interviewed John Dalton, Ray and Dave, and met various band members (sadly neither Ray nor Dave) and seen them in concert, and I consider writing a book about them to be a great honour and privilege. For the purposes of this book, I am not going into any great biographical detail – that's well-documented in other publications. But I will mention any lineup changes in the band as we go along.

As regards the actual albums, I shall concentrate on UK releases. I am aware that on occasion in the US, there were slight alterations in the running order of the albums, and different single B-sides, and I shall address them as they crop up. On some CD reissues, bonus tracks have been added. Some companies have been diligent in reissue campaigns of Kinks albums, and I'll be using the following releases for these extra tracks (which were mainly non-album singles, B-sides and EP tracks). For the Pye albums, I'll use the digitally remastered 1998 reissues on the Castle Communications label (with a few diversions into the 50th-anniversary releases on Universal), and for the RCA and Arista albums, the remastered reissues by Konk/Velvel in 1998 and 1999.

We are all aware that the band released a number of concept albums and had singles released from them. When dealing with these tracks, I shall mention a song's place in the concept when dealing with the album, but the musical side will be mentioned in the chapters dealing with the singles. As regards writers, Ray Davies composed the vast majority of songs recorded by The Kinks, but Dave Davies also contributed. So, in the following pages, if a writer is just labelled as Davies, it refers to Ray.

One last point – I realise that everyone has their own opinions about music and lyrics and I must stress that any opinions I may express are entirely my own. Are you ready to delve into the recorded output of one of the most original and innovative – not to mention influential – bands in music history? Here we go!

Formation

Formed in 1962, The Kinks went through a few changes of both lineup and name before they achieved success in 1964. The band revolved around the Davies brothers from Fortis Green, Muswell Hill – Ray (born Raymond Douglas Davies on 21 June 1944) and Dave (born David Russell Gordon Davies on 3 February 1947). For his 13th birthday, in 1957, Ray's sister Rene gave him a Spanish acoustic guitar, as he'd shown an interest in music from an early age. By 1957, Dave had also acquired a guitar: an electric one, and the brothers began to sing and play together. Another piece of the jigsaw was slotted in in 1961 when Ray met Pete Quaife. Peter Alexander Greenlaw Quaife wasn't a Londoner, having been born in Tavistock, Devon, on 31 December 1943. He and Ray met in music class, and after a short time, the idea of forming a band, took root. With both Davies brothers playing guitar, Pete took up the bass, and with his friend John Start on drums, they began rehearsing and started playing gigs. They underwent a number of name changes, from The Ray Davies Quartet to The Ravens and The Boll Weevils, and their setlist was made up of cover versions of hits and R&B songs. Ray found the mantle of lead singer uncomfortable at first, so they auditioned a few other singers. One of them was Roderick David Stewart: known as Rod. He didn't last very long as he wasn't as interested in the blues as the others were.

Early in 1963, the band entered a recording studio for the first time, but, sadly, none of these recordings exists today, and long after that, John Start decided to leave. But now that the band had the services of a booking agent and dates were planned, they lost no time in recruiting Mickey Willett. By the end of 1963, the band had management in the form of Robert Wace and Grenville Collins, with Larry Page as publishing manager. They had also sacked Mickey Willett. But most importantly, they had secured a recording contract with Louis Benjamin of Pye Records. The record company assigned Shel Talmy as their producer, and, now called The Kinks, the band entered Pye Studio 1 on 20 January 1964 and recorded five tracks with session drummer Bobby Graham.

Kinks (1964)

Personnel:
Ray Davies: rhythm guitar, piano, harmonica, lead and backing vocals
Dave Davies: lead guitar, backing and lead vocals
Pete Quaife: bass, backing vocals
Mick Avory: drums, tambourine
Additional personnel:
Rasa Didztpetris: backing vocals
Perry Ford: piano
Bobby Graham: drums
Jon Lord: Hammond organ
Arthur Greenslade: piano
Jimmy Page: 12-string guitar
Producer: Shel Talmy
Running time: 32:54
Recorded at Pye Studios 1 and 2 (January and August 1964); IBC Studios (July 1964)
Release dates: UK: 2 October 1964, US: November 1964
Original UK label and catalogue number: Pye Records NPL18096
Chart positions: UK: 3, US: 29

With the first two singles, 'Long Tall Sally' and 'You Still Want Me' failing, The Kinks' success with 'You Really Got Me' saved them, and Pye Records were naturally keen to cash in. Back in 1964 – unless you were The Beatles or Cliff Richard – success in the pop music world was considered transitory, and record companies wanted to make a quick buck while they could. So they hastily arranged a recording session for the band. At a meeting in Shel Talmy's office, Ray said that he only had about six songs written. He admitted later that in actual fact, he had loads of songs but was wondering why all the songs had to come from him, and that others should have a hand in writing. Of course, as success came and demand for his songs increased, Ray, in effect, took control of the band.

They only had four days in which to record the debut album, which would consist of 14 songs – six Ray Davies songs and eight cover versions (At the time, Ray still thought of The Kinks as mainly a covers band), all of which had been road-tested in concert. By now, The Kinks had recruited Mick Avory as their new drummer. Mick was born in Hampton Court, Surrey, as Michael Charles Avory on 15 February 1944, and at one time had been in The Rolling Stones. However, he was such a recent recruit to The Kinks that his involvement in recording the album was reduced to playing tambourine while Bobby Graham played the lion's share of the drumming.

The album cover was a simple (i.e. cheap) affair with a red-tinted image of the four band members, with the title 'Kinks' in large red letters. The back cover had sleeve notes by Brian Sommerville – The Beatles' PR man – who

9

was helping The Kinks' management at the time. They tried to come up with a gimmick to bring the band and album greater publicity and decided on an ultimately unsuccessful campaign regarding the letter K.

The album's US version was released on Frank Sinatra's Reprise label and was the same as the British release but with three tracks omitted: 'I Took My Baby Home', 'I'm A Lover Not A Fighter' and 'Revenge'.

'Beautiful Delilah' (Berry)

It's strange that the first lead vocal we hear on a Kinks album is from Dave rather than Ray. This song was played in the live shows, and Dave really gives his all. This cover of a 1968 Chuck Berry song owes more to the British beat sound rather than blues or R&B and is full of the energy The Kinks were emanating at the time.

'So Mystifying' (Davies)

The first Ray Davies lead vocal on the album is a dominant sound on his own composition, which attempts to marry the R&B style of The Rolling Stones (Dave's opening guitar riff sounds a little like their 'It's All Over Now') to vocal harmonies reminiscent of Lennon and McCartney. In 1965, Swedish band The Hep Stars released the song as a single, with future Abba member Benny Andersson on keyboards.

'Just Can't Go To Sleep' (Davies)

We've all been there: lying in bed at night thinking about our loved ones. It takes a genius like Ray Davies to actually write a song about it. Okay, he's a little obvious rhyming 'sleep' with 'counting sheep', but we don't mind: he's still learning. And dig that middle-eight with the haunting guitar sounding like Brenda Lee's 'The Crying Game'.

'Long Tall Shorty' (Covay, Abramson)

Blues singer Tommy Tucker (real name Robert Higginbotham) recorded 'Long Tall Shorty' in 1964 as his third single. It's a simple blues number with a honking harmonica that was a staple of many a band's live set, The Kinks included. And if we were in any doubt about the closeness of Ray and Dave Davies, just check out Ray's vocal: it's almost identical to Dave's on 'Beautiful Delilah'.

'I Took My Baby Home' (Davies)

The B-side to The Kink's first single 'Long Tall Sally'.
A beat-inspired song with Ray's harmonica to the fore. It didn't appear on the US release of the first album, as the first American single release had been licensed to Cameo Records. This was another track that The Larry Page Orchestra recorded for their 1965 album *Kinky Music*.

10

'I'm A Lover Not A Fighter' (Miller)

This track was missing from the original US album release but appeared on the US-only album *Kinks Size*. Written by Cajun music writer and producer J. D. 'Jay' Miller, it was first released by blues singer Lazy Lester in 1958. Featuring future Led Zeppelin guitarist Jimmy Page (an in-demand session player in 1964), this is a typical Kinks cover (or, if we want to follow the K campaign: Kinks kover).

'You Really Got Me' (Davies)

UK release: Pye Records, 7N 15673, 4 August 1964. Producer: Shel Talmy. Chart positions: UK: 1, US: 7, Australia: 8

The third single and the one that started the madness. This was The Kinks' breakthrough hit, and it nearly didn't happen. They had recorded the song in the album sessions, but in a more laid-back, bluesy style. Ray hated it and wanted to re-record it, but the record company refused. Recording manager Larry Page took Ray's side and refused to put it on the album, and Ray said he refused to promote it. This left managers Wace and Collins with a problem. If the album wasn't completed, the band would be dropped. So they stumped up the £200.00 necessary for the band to re-enter the studio and cut another version. This one worked.

Much has been written about Dave slicing his guitar-amp speaker with a razor blade to create the signature sound, which instigated decades of arguments over whether this track was the birth of heavy metal.

'Medley – Milk Cow Blues/Batman Theme /Tired Of Waiting For You/Milk Cow Blues' (Estes, Hefti, Davies, Estes)

Staring with the blues song that was on the band's third album and sung mainly by Dave, the band cuts loose a bit by sticking in an excerpt of the theme from the *Batman* TV series: which was essential viewing on Saturday and Sunday evenings in the UK at the time. We then go back to 'Milk Cow Blues', followed by the band slowing the pace for their second number one hit ', Tired Of Waiting For You'. Then the tempo ramps up again for a final bit of 'Milk Cow Blues'. Some vocals here – even though they are shouted – are lost in the maelstrom of noise. 'Thank you very much, I think you're fabulous', shouts Ray as the crowd noise fades out.

'Cadillac' (McDaniel)

Written by Elias McDaniel and recorded in 1960 under his stage name Bo Diddley, this paean to the classic American car had been in The Kinks' live set for ages. As they had played it many times, this version is as tight as it could be.

'Bald Headed Woman' (Trad. arr: Talmy)

Producer Shel Talmy managed to snag himself an arranger credit on this traditional American folk song. It's a plodding rhythm with future Deep Purple keyboardist Jon Lord filling out the sound on organ and piano. The Who and The Hep Stars recorded versions of the song in 1965.

'Revenge' (Davies, Larry Page)

A rare instrumental from the band. This was also omitted from the US release and included on the *Kinks Size* album. It has a similar guitar sound to 'You Really Got Me', with harmonica taking the place of any lyrics that Ray might've written. Page must've liked this one, as in 1965, The Larry Page Orchestra recorded it for an album of instrumental versions of Kinks songs. Easy-listening stalwart Ray McVay also recorded it the same year.

'Too Much Monkey Business' (Berry)

An energetic version of the 1956 Chuck Berry single. Again, it was a live staple of many bands, and in addition to The Kinks, The Hollies recorded it on their second album. I'll leave it to you to decide which is the better cover.

'I've Been Driving On Bald Mountain' (Trad. arr: Shel Talmy)

A traditional blues standard arranged by Shel Talmy. Ray and the boys perform an exemplary rendition with the help of Jimmy Page again.

'Stop Your Sobbin'' (Davies)

With a sound that possibly harkens back to the breakup songs of the 1950s, Ray is more subdued and emotive here. It's rumoured that he wrote it about the breakup of one of his own relationships or even about an ex-girlfriend crying about how successful he'd become. Whatever the story, it's a cracker, with plaintive vocals from Ray and some complementary harmony vocals. It certainly shows Ray's softer side.

Fifteen years later, The Pretenders recorded the song as their debut single, which led to a relationship between Ray and The Pretenders' Chrissie Hynde, ultimately resulting in Ray and Chrissie's daughter Natalie Ray Hynde.

'Got Love If You Want It' (Moore)

Slim Harpo – the master of the blues harp – recorded this song in 1957 as the B-side to 'I'm A King Bee'. He also wrote it under his real name of James Isaac Moore. With him being a leading exponent of what was termed swamp blues, the song seemed an obvious choice for The Kinks, who were heavily blues-influenced. There's a slight reverb on Ray's vocals and a superb harmonica break.

Bonus Tracks from the 1998 reissue on Castle Communications (ESM CD 482)

'Long Tall Sally' (Johnson, Penniman, Blackwell)

UK release: Pye Records, 7N 15611, 7 February 1964. Producer: Shel Talmy. Chart positions: UK: 42, US: –, Australia: –

The band's first single, as sung by Ray, and it is your typical song. In retrospect, he reckoned this cover of the Little Richard song should've been sung by Dave, as he was an expert on the American singer-songwriter.

'You Still Want Me' (Davies)

UK release: Pye Records, 7N 15636, 17 April 1964. Producer: Shel Talmy. Chart position: Did not chart

The second single was a competent beat song but didn't stand out and was poorly promoted at the time, failing to build on the number 42 placing of 'Long Tall Sally', and The Kinks were in trouble.

'You Do Something To Me' (Davies)

The B-side to the second single 'You Still Want Me'.

The intro of this B-side sounds slightly like 'You Were Made For Me' by Freddie and The Dreamers, and it's obvious that The Kinks were still cutting their teeth in both performance and writing.

'It's Alright' (Davies)

The B-side to the third single 'You Really Got Me'.

On this B-side, it seems like Ray is trying to merge blues and beat. It's perfect as a B-side or album track but probably not *pop* enough to have been considered as a contender for the A-side.

'All Day And All Of The Night' (Davies)

UK release: Pye Records, 7N 15714, 23 October 1964. Producer: Shel Talmy' Chart positions: UK: 2, US: 7, Australia: 14

The follow up to 'You Really Got Me' has a guitar riff that is similar to – and possibly inspired 'Hello I Love You' by The Doors. The lyrics about wanting to stay with your girl all night and day probably only just made it past the censors (Ray wouldn't be as lucky in 1970, as we shall see). This song also features a brilliant Dave Davies guitar solo in the middle. The Stranglers scored a number-7 hit in the UK with their version in 1988.

'I Gotta Move' (Davies)

B-side to 'All Day And All Of The Night'.

'I Gotta Move' is a riffing number, with Ray showing off a song that's both blues and up-tempo: definitely a great one for the dance floor.

Kinksize Sessions

UK release: Pye Records, NEP24200, 27 November 1964. Recorded at Pye Studios, London, 23 September 1964 and 18 October 1964. Producer: Shel Talmy. Chart position: UK: 1

'I Gotta Go Now' (Davies)

The band's first EP had four tracks that were not available on albums or singles. The opener is a softer sounding song than Kinks fans were used to, with Ray's vocal more in the front of the mix, with the instrumentation lower. Lyrically, he's trying to say goodnight to his girl, and not really wanting to.

'Things Are Getting Better' (Davies)

Another blues number, with a 'things are getting better' refrain. An up-tempo thrash that leaves the listener breathless, and the song also has a blistering harmonica break slap bang in the middle.

'I've Got That Feeling' (Davies)

Another wistful song, with piano to the fore more than in most of the songs from around this time. This song was released by The Orchids over six months before The Kinks even recorded it. The Orchids were managed by Larry Page, and were a trio of schoolgirls from Coventry. There's a story that, after a recording session, they asked Ray to lend them the fare back to Coventry, but he refused, and they had to hitchhike home.

'Louie, Louie' (Berry)

Another live staple, written by US songwriter Richard Berry. The best-known version was the 1963 hit by The Kingsmen, and this cover is almost indistinguishable from it. In total, there have been around 2,000 cover versions of this song.

'Too Much Monkey Business' (Alternate take) (Berry)

A faster and sonically more-sparse version recorded during the album sessions. Listening to both versions side by side, they were right to pick the one they did for the album as this is far too raw and the version used on the album is a bit more polished.

'I Don't Need You Any More' (Davies)

Like the alternate take of 'Too Much Monkey Business' and this song remained unreleased until this 1998 reissue. This was recorded at the band's very first studio session in January 1964, and is a pretty standard but competent beat song.

Kinda Kinks (1965)

Personnel:
Ray Davies: rhythm guitar, piano, lead and backing vocals
Dave Davies: lead guitar, backing and lead vocals
Pete Quaife: bass, backing vocals
Mick Avory: drums
Additional personnel:
Rasa Davies: backing vocals
Bobby Graham: drums
Producer: Shel Talmy
Running Time: 27:37
Recorded at Pye Studios, London (August 1964, December 1964; 15-17 February 1965)
Release dates: UK: 5 March 1965, US: 11 August 1965
Original UK label and catalogue number: Pye Records NPL18112
Chart positions: UK: 3, US: 60

The record company were keen to get the band back into the studio to record a second album, probably to build on the momentum of their early success before the bubble burst (which it wouldn't for a few more years yet). In January, the new single 'Tired Of Waiting For You' entered the charts on its way to becoming The Kinks' second number one hit, while the band were on tour on the other side of the world.

Back in December, Ray had married his girlfriend Rasa, and had to leave her behind. The tour took in Australia, New Zealand, Hong Kong and Singapore, and it was there that Ray received the news that the new single had topped the charts, and in true Ray Davies fashion, he celebrated alone. Coming home, the band had a three-day stopover in New York, where they had a hectic schedule of appearances and promotion before landing back in London on 14 February 1965. But they couldn't rest, as the next morning, they had to be in Pye Records' Studio 2 to start recording the new album – an extra pressure in that they only had three days in which to record it. As a result, the band were less than happy with it and considered it rushed.

The album cover had a band photo on grey, with the title above in blue and red 'K's. The back cover had a grainy black and white shot with a tracklisting. For the US version, 'Naggin' Woman' was left off – held over for inclusion on the *Kinkdom* album, which was an America-only release. 'Tired Of Waiting For You' and 'Come On Now' were also omitted, as they'd already appeared on the American album *Kinks Size*. The replacement tracks were 'Set Me Free' and 'Ev'rybody's Gonna Be Happy'.

'Look For Me Baby' (Davies)

The album opens with one of Ray's slower numbers. It's a song that panders to the pop sound of the era, and as such, stands up well. The lyric could arguably be Ray's take on the theme of The Hollies' 'Searchin''.

'Got My Feet On The Ground' (Ray Davies, Dave Davies)
Dave and Ray had been working on songs in their front room in Fortis Green, and Dave's input on this song – which appears to be a statement of independence – was enough to warrant a co-writing credit and lead vocal duties.

'Nothin' In The World Can Stop Me Worryin' 'Bout That Girl' (Davies)
Ray has obviously been listening to the more-folky songs that were coming to the fore at the time, and this blends that sound with a blues influence. There is some excellent finger-picking guitar work on this song.

'Naggin' Woman' (West, Anderson)
Keeping with the finger-picking guitar, this is a song written by Jay West – who is actually J. D. 'Jay' Miller (who wrote 'I'm a Lover Not A Fighter' from the first album) – and Jimmy Anderson – a blues musician, painter and preacher from Kansas City. Another lead vocal from Dave on this one.

'Wonder Where My Baby Is Tonight' (Davies)
Two lead vocals in a row for Dave, as he now fronts this piano-led rocker. You can tell, with the benefit of hindsight, how rushed the album was. Ray admitted later that the songs were better than those on the first album, but there were many mistakes made during recording that were left on the finished product, such as the double-tracking of the vocals, and this is evident throughout the album. Perhaps they should've let Ray work a bit longer on both the writing and recording.

'Tired Of Waiting For You' (Davies)
UK release: Pye Records, 7N 15759, 15 January 1965. Producer: Shel Talmy. Chart positions: UK: 1, US: 6, Australia: 29
This was recorded for the first album, but Shel Talmy left it off, as he wanted to save it for a single. Ray said he'd originally written the song on a train journey, and the final lyrics in a coffee shop during a break in recording. It was successful in other territories, too, reaching number one in South Africa, and was a top-five hit in Canada and Ireland. The jangly guitar sound is unlike the previous singles, but it showed that the band didn't have to rely on a formula to have hits. It was the last track on side one of the second album, and is the highlight of what was an otherwise mediocre album.

On The Kinks' first tour of Australia, the brothers visited their sister Rose in Adelaide, where she'd emigrated to in 1964. During the visit, she pulled out an old tape of the brothers from years before, and on it was an embryonic version of this song.

'Dancing In The Street' (Stevenson, Gaye, Hunter)

The album's second side opens with this cover of the Martha and The Vandellas hit and is one of only two tracks here not written by Ray. To be honest, it's an adequate cover but is not The Kinks' finest moment and serves as filler.

'Don't Ever Change' (Davies)

When you fall for someone, you want them to stay how they are forever – this is Ray asking his girl to stay the same. This track was already in the can, having been recorded at IBC studios the previous December.

'Come On Now' (Davies)

B-side of 'Tired of Waiting'.
This B-side had lead vocals courtesy of Dave Davies, and was an upbeat rocker. It was recorded at Pye Studios a couple of days before Christmas 1964.

'So Long' (Davies)

Ray has always had a way with words, and this is him saying goodbye in his own inimitable style. It's a rather a folky number with great harmonies, and it wouldn't have been out of place on a Simon & Garfunkel album.

'You Shouldn't Be Sad' (Davies)

You can't always tell if Ray's lyrics come from his own experiences, as he was at the time rather introverted and was known to live vicariously through his more outgoing brother. This beat song is telling us that he's '...in paradise/I feel alright/I feel okay 'cause I'm in love', and that we shouldn't be sad about that.

With Ray's lead vocal and the group's answering chorus, this sounds a little 'Beatle-esque' to my ears – bit a lot rougher.

'Something Better Beginning' (Davies)

This lyric seems to suggest that when you ask a girl to dance for the first time, you wonder whether this will be the beginning of something better. This song closed the album, and wasn't considered as a single for The Kinks. However, The Honeycombs took it into the top 40 in the UK in 1965. Recorded at the same session as 'Don't Ever Change', the guitar is in the back of the mix but is reminiscent of the jangly sound of 'See My Friends'.

Bonus Tracks from the 1998 reissue on Castle Communications (ESM CD 483)

'Ev'rybody's Gonna Be Happy' (Davies)

Single A-side. UK release: Pye Records, 7N 15813, 19 March 1965. Producer: Shel Talmy. Chart positions: UK: 17, US: –, Australia: –
Ray said that this A-side was inspired by Earl Van Dyle's Motown band with whom The Kinks had toured. It was recorded in the same session as 'Come

On Now'. Apparently, drummer Mick Avory found it difficult to play, as the rhythm was complex.

After two chart-toppers and a number two hit, this single was a relative failure, but the band would bounce back.

'Who'll Be The Next In Line' (Davies)

B-side of 'Ev'rybody's Gonna Be Happy'.

This B-side was recorded at the same session as the A-side. Ray seems to be castigating (in his own way) a woman after dumping him (which may or may not be based on real-life events). He's telling her that he's the best one she'll ever have.

'Set Me Free' (Davies)

Single A-side. UK release: Pye Records, 7N 15854, 21 May 1965. Producer: Shel Talmy. Chart positions: UK: 9, US: 23, Australia: 54

Recorded on 13 April 1965 at Pye Studios, this was another top ten single, and had its origins in the days when Ray and Dave played as a duo in clubs. It has a rolling guitar riff and uncomplicated lyrics.

'I Need You' (Davies)

B-side of 'Set Me Free'.

This B-side also has simple lyrics, and is very listenable. Recording started on 13 April 1965, and was completed the day after.

'See My Friends' (Davies)

Single A-side. UK release: Pye Records, 7N 15919, 30 July 1965. Producer: Shel Talmy. Chart positions: UK: 10, US: –, Australia: –

At the same two-day session as the previous single tracks, The Kinks recorded yet another hit. The eastern drone came through a happy accident – Dave had an old 12-string Framus guitar, and when played in the studio too near to the microphone, the feedback created the drone.

'Never Met A Girl Like You Before' (Davies)

B-side of 'See My Friends'.

This flip side intro teases us with the intro of 'Tired Of Waiting For You' and then launches into an up-tempo song. Lyrically, Ray is extolling the virtues of the girl in question.

Kwyet Kinks EP

UK release: Pye Records, NEP24221, 17 Sept 1965. Recorded April, June and August 1965. Producer: Shel Talmy. Chart position: UK: 1

'Wait Till The Summer Comes Along' (Dave Davies)

As with the *Kinksize Sessions* EP, the four tracks on *Kwyet Kinks* were exclusive to the release and unavailable at the time on album or single. The lead track was written and sung by Dave, and his acoustic guitar is prominent with a jolly country feel.

'Such A Shame' (Davies)

According to the lyric, Ray feels he's let someone down and is expressing his regret. To be honest, it's a pretty unspectacular slow number.

'A Well Respected Man' (Davies)

Ray would have plenty of social commentary on later albums, but this is regarded as the first example of it. This track appeared on the American *Kinkdom* album. Pye Records didn't want to release it as a single because they wanted one with more-raunchy songs. But it was good enough, as evidenced by its performance abroad.

Released as a single in the US and continental Europe, it reached number nine in the US *Cashbox* chart and went top ten in Canada, Sweden, Malaysia, Holland, Singapore and South Africa.

In 1965, Petula Clark released a cover version sung in French, which caused slight consternation in America with the use of the word 'fag': meaning cigarettes.

'Don't You Fret' (Davies)

This could almost be a hymn, with the acoustic guitar and organ, with Ray saying not to fret as he'll be there to hold your hand. After the first verse, we get a more 'pop' sound, albeit at a slow tempo.

'I Go To Sleep' (Demo) (Davies)

This is Ray's demo recording, accompanying himself on piano. It was never recorded by The Kinks. The Applejacks were one of the first to record it and released it as a single in August 1965. Cher and Peggy Lee also recorded it that year, and it is still regularly covered. The Pretenders took it to number seven in the UK charts in 1981.

The Kink Kontroversy (1965)

Personnel:
Ray Davies: rhythm guitar, harmonica, lead and backing vocals
Dave Davies: lead guitar, backing and lead vocals
Pete Quaife: bass, backing vocals
Mick Avory: drums, tambourine
Additional personnel:
Rasa Davies: backing vocals
Clem Cattini: drums
Nicky Hopkins: keyboards
Shel Talmy: guitar
Producer: Shel Talmy
Running Time: 30:12
Recorded at Pye Studios, London (23-30 October 1965)
Original UK label and catalogue number: Pye Records NPL18131
Release dates: UK: 26 November 1965, US: March 1966
Chart positions: UK: 9, US: 95

The bands' third album would be (thankfully) the last to play with the letter K. Their profile had been kept high throughout the year with single releases and touring. But behind the scenes, things were happening. Some of the band relationships had been a bit fractious, and things boiled over from time to time. The Davies brothers were often at loggerheads, Pete Quaife was becoming frustrated that his ideas were being ignored, and the relationship between Dave Davies and drummer Mick Avory almost caused police involvement. During a May tour, the pair had fought, leading to Dave going on stage the next night wearing sunglasses hiding two black eyes. However, the worst incident took place in Cardiff, where Mick hit Dave with his drum pedal, leaving the guitarist out cold on stage and covered in blood. Mick fled the scene, not knowing whether he'd killed Dave or not. But things were resolved in the end (although, in the 1980s, more differences with Dave would lead to Mick leaving the band, but more about that later).

The band then went on a tour of America. Ray was reluctant to go, as his daughter Louisa had just been born, but, in the end, he agreed to. On tour, disagreements with union officials led to Ray punching one of them, and overall – for the Davies brothers especially – it wasn't a happy tour. It also didn't help that Larry Page – who had gone with them – left them in the middle of the tour and returned to England.

America had just gone through the first wave of the British invasion and was getting worried that British bands were taking over. Ray thinks they were looking for a reason to start banning bands from touring America, and the incident with the union official was just the excuse they needed. The Kinks essentially got banned from playing in America from 1965 to 1969. Whilst, on the one hand this was financially disastrous, it meant that Ray had to turn towards England for his inspiration, and this would lead to some of his greatest songs. Added to all this was the fact that the management team was also falling out. And to cut a long (and complicated) story short, the original publishing deal the band had with Denmark Productions and Kassner Music was broken, and the band formed their own company called Belinda, with Carlin Music. The ensuing litigation meant that Carlin had to put all monies in escrow, which means it was placed in trust until everything was sorted out. So Ray got no money from his songs – apart from airplay royalties – until it was sorted in 1970.

Because of all this, releases were delayed, and it would be October 1965 before the band entered the studio to record *The Kink Kontroversy* – but this time, they were given a whole week! Even though they had a little more time to record, the budget was still paltry when compared to that of, say, The Beatles. But the band had been upgrading their instruments. Dave had bought a Gibson Flying V guitar in America, and other guitars now included a Gretsch and acoustic Fenders.

Of the dozen tracks, ten were written by Ray and one by Dave. The sole cover version was the album opener 'Milk Cow Blues'. It was also the first Kinks album on which the UK and US track listings were identical. Ray felt pressured when writing the album, as it was now generally accepted that he was the band's main songwriter. During a particularly bad patch, managers Wace and Collins persuaded top US songwriter Mort Shuman (who had co-written hits like 'Can't Get Used To Losing You', 'Viva Las Vegas' and 'Teenager In Love') to visit Ray and give him a pep talk. It worked, and Ray came up with the two Kinks' classics 'Till The End Of The Day' and 'Where Have All The Good Times Gone'.

The album cover had the title and four small portraits of the band members above a larger image of Dave's guitar. On the back was the tracklisting and a few paragraphs written by Michel Aldred – one of the hosts of the influential Rediffusion TV show *Ready Steady Go!*, and who for a time shared a house with Dave and Mick (although, given their volatile relationship, I often wonder why Dave and Mick would share a house).

'Milk Cow Blues' (John Adam 'Sleepy Joe' Estes)
This track featured in The Kinks' live set for some time and was originally recorded by blues musician Kokomo Arnold in 1934 (and who would also record four sequels over the next two years). Session man extraordinaire Clem Cattini, who was a member of Joe Meek's recording band The Tornados and also Billy Fury's live band, is on the drum stool for this one, and Ray and Dave share the lead vocal. Check out Pete Quaife's bass line near the end – he later said that he was 'showing off' and wanted the bass to sound more like a lead instrument.

'Ring The Bells' (Davies)
On the US tour, Larry Page arranged a recording session in Los Angeles, and recorded the demo for this song which he hoped would be a single (though it

would later lead to him being ousted from the band's management team). It's a softer number, with Cattini drumming again. The amazing acoustic guitar does actually sound like bells.

'Gotta Get The First Plane Home' (Davies)
Feelings of despair leak into some of this album's songs, and this is one of them. It was probably influenced by Ray's less-than-happy American tour experiences and addresses his homesickness. It harkens back to The Kinks' earlier sound with Nicky Hopkins' piano well to the fore. Ray also plays some strong blues harp.

'When I See That Girl Of Mine' (Davies)
A happier number with a big beat influence, reminiscent (to your author) of a Beatles/Searchers hybrid. Ray is telling us how happy he is when he sees his girl. But is he talking about wife Rasa or new daughter Louisa?

'I Am Free' (Dave Davies)
This is the album's sole Dave-written track, and has him doing lead vocals too. It's a Dylanesque song, by which I mean that similar to Bob Dylan, Dave is almost speaking his lyrics rather than singing them to the melody. Lyrically, Dave appears to be singing about his freedom to pursue the hedonistic lifestyle he was enjoying at the time.

'Till The End Of The Day' (Davies)
Single A-side. UK release: Pye Records, 7N 15981, 19 November 1965. Producer: Shel Talmy. Chart positions: UK: 6, US: 50, Australia: 63
This powerful A-side – similar in sound to earlier hits – is about escape and freedom. It was based on power chords thanks to the pep talk given to Ray by songwriter Mort Shuman, who suggested picking chords Ray liked and building a song around them. It reached the top ten in the UK, Netherlands, Norway and Sweden.

'The World Keeps Going Round' (Davies)
Side two kicks off with this song about isolation and powerlessness. Ray is saying what's the use of worrying as the world will just keep on turning. The guitar and drum intro has a hint of psychedelia, predating that genre by a good twelve months.

'I'm On An Island' (Davies)
This faux calypso song again emanates a feeling of isolation. Or is it wishful thinking? It's okay to be on an island as long as he's got his girl with him. Could he have caught an episode of *Desert Island Discs*?

'Where Have All The Good Times Gone' (Davies)

B-side to 'Till The End Of The Day'.

Ray was becoming a bit disillusioned with having to be away from home a lot. The band had been successful, but he wasn't happy, and this song was his comment about that fact. It's another track resulting from the Mort Shuman talk and again features Clem Cattini on drums.

Davies was 21 when he wrote the song, but he sounds 40. He explained he was taking inspiration from older people around him. But more importantly, it showed he could *become* a character, and this would be important in later years.

'It's Too Late' (Davies)

When you say something you didn't mean, it's too late to take it back, and that is what this song is about. Shel Talmy plays guitar on this track which has a short but effective piano break in the middle. If Status Quo had been doing their 12-bar shuffle back in 1965, it would more than likely have sounded like this.

'What's In Store For Me' (Davies)

Ray was keeping his titles and lyrics simple at this point, and this is no exception. Dave is singing the lead on this song which could be regarded as Ray's version of the Doris Day standard 'Que Sera Sera' from the movie *The Man Who Knew Too Much*, where the singer is asking what is to become of them in the future.

'You Can't Win' (Davies)

Ray and Dave share the lead vocal here, expressing the despair that no matter how many times you try, you can't win in the end, and this reaffirms the themes of desolation and futility that make up a fair proportion of the album. The subject matter might be a bit downbeat, but it's a good song to finish the album on.

Bonus Tracks from the 1998 reissue on Castle Communications (ESM CD 507)

'Dedicated Follower Of Fashion' (Davies)

UK release: Pye Records, 7N 17064, 25 February 1966. Producer: Shel Talmy. Chart positions: UK: 4, US: 36, Australia: 36

Ray wrote this song following a fight he had with a fashion designer at a party. The following day, he decided to channel his anger into lyrics, and this satirical swipe at the fashionistas of the day was the result. It was recorded between 7 and 10 February 1966 at Pye Studios, and try as he might, he was never happy with the intro. Dave didn't like the song at all, and many people said it had its musical origins in the English music hall tradition.

But the record was one of the most successful. Top five in Britain, it also reached the top 10 in Denmark, Canada, Ireland, Norway and Singapore, and topped the charts in The Netherlands and New Zealand. The lyric also netted Ray an Ivor Novello Award for songwriting.

'Sittin' On My Sofa' (Ray Davies, Dave Davies)
B-side to 'Dedicated Follower Of Fashion'.
Ray's writing was by now heading away from the American R&B sound on which the band had their early foundations and was becoming more English, but 'Sittin' On My Sofa' has a definite bluesy feel. Nobody likes just sitting around waiting for something to happen, and this is Ray's comment on that. It was recorded at Pye Studios in December 1965.

'When I See That Girl Of Mine' (Demo) (Davies)
This demo of the album track was recorded back in May 1965 at Regent Sound Studio. It sounds quite different from the album version.

'Dedicated Follower Of Fashion' (Stereo alternate take) (Davies)
The band were still recording in mono at the time but managed to achieve this stereo take of the single. It's strange not hearing the 'Oh yes he is' refrain. It was recorded at the album sessions.

Face To Face (1966)

Personnel:
Ray Davies: rhythm guitar, mellotron, lead vocals
Dave Davies: lead guitar, backing and lead vocals
Pete Quaife: bass, backing vocals
Mick Avory: drums, percussion
Additional personnel:
Rasa Davies: backing vocals
John Dalton: bass, backing vocals
Nicky Hopkins: keyboards, piano, harmonium
Producer: Shel Talmy
Running time: 38:32
Recorded at Pye Studios, London (October and December 1965, May and June 1966, January 1966, April-June 1966)
Release dates: UK: 28 October 1966, US: 7 December 1966
Original UK label and catalogue number: Pye Records NPL18149
Chart positions: UK: 12, US: 135

As the initial burst of activity began to slow down, album releases became annual events, and there was a wait of 11 months before the new album. (In the future, the only year in which we had two new Kinks albums was 1971, but one of them was the *Percy* soundtrack). Despite this, 1966 was an eventful year for the band, with two UK hits (one of them a chart-topper) and tours. The band also had their first lineup changes: albeit temporarily.

In March, they embarked on a ten-day tour of Belgium without Ray. After earlier shows in Denmark, Switzerland and Austria, the singer was exhausted, and Dave had to take over his press duties. But the tour of Belgium had to go ahead. Ray picked his own replacement – Mick Grace of The Cockneys – who was ordered to bluff his way through and keep his head down. With Dave handling the vocals, the band just about got away with it. However, this was just the start of Ray's problems. He was becoming increasingly paranoid, and following a phone argument with the band's publicist Brian Sommerville, he ran across London just to punch him (apparently, he missed). Sommerville resigned.

To help Ray calm down, Robert Wace took him for a drive outside the city, and Ray became enamoured with the idea of buying a house in the country and subsequently wrote a song about it. He also began writing quieter songs in order to not disturb his family while they slept.

When Ray returned to live performances after a six-week break, Mick Avory was absent for a few shows after coming down with tonsilitis, and stalwart Clem Cattini filled in for him. Then on 4 May 1966, on his way home from a gig in Morecambe, bassist Pete Quaife was involved in a road accident that left him unable to work. With promotional work for the new single 'Sunny Afternoon' to be undertaken, and shows lined up, the band – thanks to their booking agent Arthur Howes – found a temporary replacement in John Dalton (born 21 May 1943 in Chipping Barnet, London). John had just left the band Mark Four and was delivering coal for a living when he auditioned on 9 June. He was accepted, and that same night recorded *Top Of The Pops*: the band lip-synching to 'Sunny Afternoon'. After some to-ing and fro-ing, Pete Quaife returned to the band in November, and Dalton returned to his day job

Face To Face contains 14 songs, all from the pen of Ray Davies, marking the first time that he wrote a whole album. At the time, he called it 'a collection of songs' and attempted to provide some cohesion by adding sound effects. Pye didn't like this idea and vetoed it. However, three made it onto the album. It has been argued that this was The Kinks' first concept album, having a common theme of social observation. Gone was the raucousness of the first three albums – this is a gentler record, and more melodic than what had gone before. Another new feature was that the band hadn't had to thrash it out in a few days in the studios. Part of the delay in releasing the new album was due to the band having discussions to renew their Pye contract. The new contract would run for five years.

The cover was a departure too. Minus a band picture, there was a seemingly psychedelic painting of a man's head (looking like something out of *Monty Python*) with butterflies coming out of it. Ray didn't like it – he wanted something strong and black and not psychedelic, as it didn't represent the music. The back cover had a track listing, a monochrome version of the man's head, and some sleeve notes by publicist Frank Smyth using lyrics to form the notes.

'Party Line' (Davies)

In Dave's 1996 autobiography *Kink*, he claims that he wrote this and Ray helped him out. Some album covers list it as a co-write. We'll probably never know for certain unless we get the two of them into a room and grill them.

Party lines on phones were the bane of many people's lives (see the film *Pillow Talk* with Doris Day and Rock Hudson), and Dave as lead vocalist, is complaining about his party line. This jaunty song includes one of the three surviving sound effects that Ray wanted to populate the album with: a telephone ringing. The phone is answered by band manager Grenville Collins.

The song was a B-side to 'Dandy' in some countries, and in others – such as Norway – it was switched to the A-side.

'Rosie Won't You Please Come Home' (Davies)

When Ray and Dave's sister Rose – along with her husband Arthur Anning – emigrated to Adelaide, Australia, in 1964, Ray was particularly upset, as he was very close to her, and this song is a plea for her to return home. The song has a lovely harpsichord sound.

Rose's husband Arthur would become the Arthur immortalised in The Kinks' 1969 album of the same name.

'Dandy' (Davies)

This song, very much in the English music hall tradition, is allegedly about Dave's lifestyle, as seen through Ray's eyes. It was released as a single in Europe, hitting the top ten in Austria, Belgium and Holland, and hitting the very top in Germany. Herman's Hermits cover version topped the Canadian charts and went top five in the US. The Rockin' Vickers – another Shel-Talmy-produced band – also recorded the song. The band's guitarist was Ian Kilmister, then known as Ian Willis, and later as Lemmy.

'Too Much On My Mind' (Davies)

This quiet and reflective song is one from Ray's heart and mind. It expresses his fragile mental state at the time. The acoustic guitar and harpsichord make an unbeatable musical team on this track.

'Session Man' (Davies)

The Kinks employed a few session musicians in the studios, and this song is about them. It was probably most inspired by keyboard player Nicky Hopkins, who has always been regarded as one of the very best. The lyrics perfectly sum up the role of session men, and despite the fact that a session man is 'not paid to think, just play' Ray does say that he (Hopkins?) is a 'top' musician. And the opening harpsicord emphasises this fact.

'Rainy Day In June' (Davies)

Another atmospheric number from Ray, which included the sound effect of thunder. He's not just telling us about a rainy day in summer (Definition of an English summer? Three sunny days followed by a thunderstorm); he's effectively using the storm after nice weather as a metaphor for describing his moods.

'A House In The Country' (Davies)

This lyrics on this upbeat number were inspired by the calming drive in the country that Robert Wace took Ray on after his aforementioned meltdown with Brian Sommerville. However, Ray can't help putting in a jibe about the rich. The Pretty Things had a minor hit (number 50) with their version in the summer of 1966.

'Holiday On Waikiki' (Davies)

The last of the sound effects are of waves lapping onto the beach, as we have a story from Ray about someone winning the holiday in a newspaper. Once there, though, the winner is disappointed at the amount of commercialisation. Even in his happier songs, Ray can't resist getting a barb in somewhere. Honestly, Ray would probably be able to have a dig at Christmas – see 1977 and 'Father Christmas'!

'Most Exclusive Residence For Sale' (Davies)

Another swipe at the rich. This time the protagonist is already rich, but then suffers the transience of fortune as he wastes his wealth and goes bankrupt. This is a strong song from the band, opening with a punchy guitar and bass and is a 'cautionary tale' highlighting the fact that you can lose everything if you're not careful.

'Fancy' (Davies)

Written late one night on an old Framus guitar which was able to sustain notes like an Indian tambura drone, the song is like a mantra. Ray stated that it was about perception, but to me, the lyrics suggest he is building mental walls that we can't break down.

'Little Miss Queen Of Darkness' (Davies)

A little song about a dancer in a discotheque being very friendly on the outside – but beware, she is out for what she can get. Mick Avory said he contributed a lot to this (and the outro to 'Holiday In Waikiki') as he was starting to listen more to the music and getting to grips with Ray's methods.

'You're Lookin' Fine' (Davies)

A second lead vocal from Dave, and he's being complimentary about a girl's looks. This song was written and recorded before the main writing sessions and is a little more basic, therefore it seems a little out of place on the album.

'Sunny Afternoon' (Davies)

Single A-side. UK release: Pye Records, 7N 17125, 3 June 1966. Producer: Shel Talmy. Chart positions: UK: 1, US: 14, Australia: 13

Ray's rant against the taxman topped the UK charts for two weeks in July 1966, and was successful almost everywhere, topping the charts in Canada, The Netherlands, Ireland and Norway. It also went top ten in Finland, Germany, New Zealand and Spain, and was the eighth best-selling single in the UK that year: going Silver with sales of over 250,000. This is one of The Kinks' career highlights, and rightly so, as it defines the summer of 1966 (Okay, England winning the World Cup might do so as well). Ray's narrative tells us that money can't buy everything, especially if you're drunk, and cruel to your girlfriend.

'I'll Remember' (Davies)

This was the first track to be recorded for the album, back in October 1965. A fairly simple beat song about a breakup. Some great thudding bass from Pete Quaife punctuates this song throughout.

Bonus Tracks from the 1998 reissue on Castle Communications (ESM CD 479)

'I'm Not Like Everybody Else' (Davies)

B-side of 'Sunny Afternoon'.

This Dave-sung B-side is a statement of nonconformity. It starts fairly quietly but builds to a screaming crescendo. The song was offered to The Animals to record, but they turned it down.

'Dead End Street' (Davies)

Single A-side. UK release: Pye Records, 7N 17222, 18 November 1966. Producer: Shel Talmy. Chart positions: UK: 5, US: 73, Australia: 62

This comment on poverty has a black and white film to accompany it, with the band as undertakers picking up a coffin. The dark subject matter didn't win any fans at the BBC, and the film was promptly banned. But the tale of poverty struck a chord, and it was a big hit. It was also a top ten hit in Canada, Germany, The Netherlands, Ireland, New Zealand and Norway. It was recorded in October 1966 with John Dalton and Dave Davies playing two bass guitars. Pete Quaife appeared in the film, though. The Kinks-influenced band The Jam covered it.

'Big Black Smoke' (Davies)

B-side to 'Dead End Street'.

'Big Black Smoke' was the perfect B-side, as it had similar themes. It could've been influenced by the groundbreaking television play *Cathy Come Home.* The song tells the story of a runaway from the country to the city, where she ends up living rough and taking drugs. Yes, there is a controversial reference to drugs, as she 'spends her money on purple hearts'.

'Mister Pleasant' (Davies)

B-side to future single 'Autumn Almanac', and a single in Europe and the USA

'Mr. Pleasant' had seen release as an A-side in the US and Europe. America was keen on these music hall novelty songs (although the satire about the complacency of the rich might have been lost in translation), as evidenced by Hermans' Hermits having number one hits there with 'I'm Henry VIII, I Am' and 'Mrs. Brown, You've Got A Lovely Daughter'. There's a little bit of trombone in there and some ragtime piano courtesy of Nicky Hopkins.

'This Is Where I Belong' (Davies)

As 'Mister Pleasant' was released as a single in Europe, this was the B-side. It was recorded probably for inclusion on the *Face To Face* album but was ultimately left off it. It's one of Ray's more emotionally-upbeat songs, as he's effectively telling us that he's happy with his lot and there's nowhere he would rather be.

'Mr. Reporter' (Davies)

This song was written for an unreleased EP titled *Occupation*. But the track wasn't released, as the record company thought it might antagonise the press. There's a nice uncredited brass section lurking in there too.

'Little Women' (Backing track) (Davies)

An unreleased backing track recorded at Pye Studios for a song that was never finished. It's a very pleasant piece with woodwind in the background, hinting at The Beatles' 'Strawberry Fields Forever'. Towards the end, we get Nicky Hopkins on Mellotron. I think – after 54 years – Ray should go back and complete it.

Other contemporary track
'She's Got Everything' (Davies)

B-side to single 'Days' in both the UK and US.

Recorded in February 1966 during the Face To Face sessions. It was left off that album and the next one. The song is definitely from the bands' early period, as is evidenced in the 'garage' sound of the guitar and the simplicity of the lyrics.

This track appeared on a couple of later compilations but was never played live by The Kinks; however, Dave Davies featured the song regularly in his solo sets in the nineties and early noughties. And there is a live version on his 2000 CD, *Rock Bottom Live*.

Something Else By The Kinks (1967)

Personnel:
Ray Davies: rhythm guitar, harmonica, harp, harpsichord, organ, tuba, maracas, lead vocals
Dave Davies: lead guitar, 12-string guitar, backing and lead vocals
Pete Quaife: bass, backing vocals
Mick Avory: drums, percussion
Additional personnel:
Rasa Davies: backing vocals
Nicky Hopkins: keyboards, piano
Producers: Shel Talmy, Ray Davies
Running Time: 36:17
Recorded at Pye Studios, London (April 1966; November 1966 to February 1967; spring and June 1967)
Release dates: UK: 15 September 1967, US: January 1968
Original UK label and catalogue number: Pye Records NPL18193
Chart positions: UK: 35, US: 153

1967 was a quiet year for The Kinks as regards singles, with only two being released in the UK – both classics, though, and one of them destined to become a defining record of the decade. We also have the start of Dave Davies' solo career (in fact, he released the same number of singles in the UK as the band).

The Kinks continued to tour, which is more than what The Beatles were doing, as they gave up live performances the previous year. In between tours, Ray was working on new material with renewed vigour after his problems, and both Dave and Pete got married. The fact that the band couldn't go to America to perform, meant that Ray went even more English in his outlook, and the 1967 album *Something Else By The Kinks* was steeped in influences of his home country.

We would have to wait until September for the release of the new album, but before then, a lot happened in the Davies' Kinkdom. On 1 April 1967, the band and assorted engineers drove up to Scotland and recorded the band's first live album (more about which later), and no sooner had they returned than they convened in Pye Studios to record what is possibly Ray's greatest song: 'Waterloo Sunset'. The same month that the single peaked in the charts – in fact, on 13 May 1967 – Ray announced he was leaving the band to concentrate on writing on producing: doing what Brian Wilson did in The Beach Boys. Ray retracted his statement three days later.

Something Else By The Kinks hit British record shops in September, whilst America had to wait until January 1968 (A reverse of the live album, which was released in America in August 1967 and the UK in January 1968). The 13 tracks (obviously, nobody was superstitious) contain some of Ray's greatest observations and stories, and as such, it deserved a better chart showing.

Subsequent years have been kinder to this record, as more and more people started to really listen to it. Unfortunately, it stalled in the UK charts at 35 and, amazingly, was the last original Kinks album to chart in their homeland. They would have eight more entries in the album chart, all of them compilations with the first one *Sunny Afternoon* (a budget-priced collection released on Marble Arch Records in December 1967), having the distinction of being the final Kinks album to reach the top 10. The reasons for the poor performance could have included that happier records were dominating the charts at the time. The Beatles had released *Sgt. Pepper's Lonely Hearts Club Band* in June, and The Monkees – the latest craze from America – had released three albums so far this year: two chart-toppers and a third, which only made it to number two. It managed to scrape to 153 in America, where promotion – thanks to their ban – was non-existent.

The cover to *Something Else* is the worst in The Kinks' canon. It was mainly purple with darker purple etchings of the band members. The uncredited sleeve notes ramble, and talk about Daviesland where all the 'kinklings' are typically English. I think the writer is trying to be a little psychedelic in outlook, but it just doesn't fit. More importantly for the band's future, this would be the last time Shel Talmy would have a hand in recording. In truth, the album was mainly produced by Ray, who also had a hand in the mixing. It also features three writing credits for Dave: more than on any other Kinks album.

'David Watts' (Davies)

With Dave's studio chatter intro of 'Nice and smooth', Ray partly based this iconic and sardonic song on both a promoter who had propositioned Dave at a post-gig party at his house, and the typical high-achiever at school who everybody wanted to be like. Dave didn't fancy the promoter, but he remained friends with the band. Musically it's a stomping rocker, which would be covered by mod revivalists The Jam, who charted with it in 1978. The song was also the B-side to 'Autumn Almanac' in the US and Europe.

'Death Of A Clown' (Davies, Dave Davies)

This was released as a Dave Davies solo single. I have included it here as an album track. The distinctive intro was created by Ray plucking the piano strings. Lyrically, it's a lament about the repetitive recording and touring schedule. Dave was also becoming disillusioned with partying and being the life and soul of the party.

'Two Sisters' (Davies)

A harpsichord-heavy song about two sisters: Sybilla who is a 'wayward lass' and Priscilla who is a married housewife. Nothing is ever straightforward with Ray, and he has admitted that *he* is Priscilla and Dave is Sybilla. The song reflects the difference between the two brothers, as both sisters are jealous of each other. Deep down, perhaps Ray was jealous of the fact that Dave was more outgoing and comfortable around people; but Ray being Ray, had to get in the fact that Dave could equally have been jealous of Ray's talent. This song marks the first use of strings on a Kinks track. It was the B-side of 'Waterloo Sunset' in the US.

'No Return' (Davies)
Ray is having a go at a bossa nova song here, with some lovely acoustic guitar. If The Kinks decided to do an easy-listening compilation, this would have to be on it. Lyrically, it's a sad song about the end of a relationship.

'Harry Rag' (Davies)
'Harry Rag' is a cockney rhyming slang term for a fag (in the UK, a cigarette), a reference to the jockey Harry Wragg, and was a phrase Ray's dad used ('And rolls himself a Harry Rag'). It's a jaunty piece in the music hall tradition and could've been inspired by the sing-alongs around the piano at the Davies' family home.

'Tin Soldier Man' (Davies)
'Two Sisters' has strings, and this one also has a brass section. This song is one of Ray's allegorical commentaries on the fact that all city gentlemen look the same, with the same style of clothes, and everything in their life conforming: even their wives.

'Situation Vacant' (Davies)
A domestic vignette about Johnny leaving his comfortable job, as his mother-in-law thinks he should be more ambitious. Sadly, despite reading the situations vacant columns, he's unable to get a new job and loses everything. It's seemingly an upbeat song, yet the clashing chords at the end betray its darkness.

'Love Me Till The Sun Shines' (Dave Davies)
B-side to 'Death Of A Clown'. A love song of sorts with a bit of a twist. Dave is telling the object of his affections that she doesn't have to share anything with him, and can even take all his money as long as she loves him. The song is a little 'proggy' as it settles into a crunchy bass and low-register guitar-led track.

'Lazy Old Sun' (Davies)
A dark allegory about the end of summer – Ray has a fascination with autumn and would return to the topic on several occasions. He once said that autumn was his favourite season. The confused sound reflects the depression of the protagonist, who is bemoaning the fact that the sun isn't strong enough to brighten his life. Another nod towards the coming psychedelic and progressive era with deep bass and a little brass – followed by organ.

'Afternoon Tea' (Davies)

Another story song from Ray about missing his girl Donna, though we don't know if Donna is a real person or not. Apparently, his happy memories of her include the times when they partook of afternoon tea together. Ray is already looking at the type of song he would be utilising in his 'Village Green' concept, with music that is not too harsh or soft, with the lyrics to the fore.

'Funny Face' (Dave Davies)

The B-side to Dave's second solo single. It's generally regarded as a song about a woman's terminal illness and how, as the illness takes hold, it affects her looks. Dave uses the metaphor of makeup being smudged. Despite its subject matter, the song moves along at a fair lick.

'End Of The Season' (Davies)

Ray's fascination with autumn continues with this shuffle about the onset of winter. He appears to be attempting a crooning style of singing here. Juxtaposed to that are birdsong effects.

'Waterloo Sunset' (Davies)

Single A-side. UK release: Pye Records, 7N 17321, 5 May 1967. Producer: Ray Davies. Chart positions: UK: 2, US: –, Australia: 4

This single A-side that was a tribute to London. Ray had walked over the bridge often when at art school and had seen the area many times as a child in hospital. For the past four years, the music scene seemed to be centred on Liverpool, but Ray wanted to write a quintessentially London-influenced song. He said that he woke up singing it in his sleep like Frank Sinatra.

Ray admitted later that the band went into the studio and recorded this without Shel Talmy's knowledge. It has always been surmised that the Terry and Julie characters were meant to be Terence Stamp and Julie Christie, who were among the top actors of the time. However, Ray has said that he didn't have them in mind when he wrote the song. But he told journalist Keith Altham that if the song was a film, then Stamp and Christie would *have* to play them.

Bonus Tracks from the 1998 reissue on Castle Communications (ESM CD 480)

'Act Nice And Gentle' (Ray Davies)

B-side to 'Waterloo Sunset'

On this B-side, Ray is telling us that it doesn't matter how you're dressed or how showy you are; he is happy when you 'act nice and gentle' and be polite. He is perhaps commenting on the fact that good manners were fast disappearing. It's almost country and western in style, with a hint of Mungo Jerry; all it needs is a jug band.

'Autumn Almanac' (Davies)

Single A-side. UK release: Pye Records, 7N 17400, 13 October 1967. Producer: Ray Davies. Chart positions: UK: 3, US: –, Australia: 73

Recorded at Pye Studios in March 1967, 'Autumn Almanac' reached the top 10 in the Netherlands, Belgium, Malaysia and Singapore and this study of working-class English life got to number three in the UK and is based on Ray's real-life gardener. There's a hint of nostalgia for simpler times, and the lyrics resonated with almost everyone in that class strata – 'Roast beef on Sundays', 'I go to Blackpool for my holidays', 'Football on a Saturday'. Yes, they were a part of our lives, and though I doubt very much that Ray Davies ever went to Blackpool for a holiday, *I* did. But that's because Blackpool was mainly an English seaside resort favoured by working-class people from the north and middle parts of England. Ray, being from London, would probably have gone to the south coast or Essex.

'Susannah's Still Alive' (Dave Davies)

This is Dave's second solo single, which got to 20 in the UK, 10 in The Netherlands, and reached the top 20 in Belgium and Sweden. It has a strong piano and bass riff throughout. Susannah is missing her lover from years past: so much so that she is slowly drinking herself to death. Sadly, this was Dave's final solo chart appearance in the UK.

'Wonderboy' (Ray Davies)

Single A-side. UK release: Pye Records, 7N 17468, 5 April 1968. Producer: Ray Davies. Chart positions: UK: 36, US: –, Australia: –

This A-side was a relative failure, only reaching 36 in the UK (their lowest chart placing since the first two singles). However, it reached 6 in the Netherlands, where The Kinks could do no wrong. John Lennon said he liked it, but Peter Quaife hated it. The song is about looking at a child for the first time and wondering what his life will be like, and was written after the birth of Ray and Rasa's second daughter Victoria.

'Polly' (Ray Davies)

B-side to 'Wonderboy'.

This B-side is sometimes called 'Pretty Polly': a story of a teenage girl's rebellion. She runs off to the big city, but in the end, returns home. Her mother understands as *she* wanted to do the same thing when she was younger. The 'oooh's' on the background could be by The Who, they sound so much like The Kinks' London rivals.

'Lincoln County' (Dave Davies)

Dave's third solo single. It reached 15 in The Netherlands, but despite good airplay on BBC's Radio One, it failed to chart in Britain. In the song, the protagonist has been in jail but is now returning home. However, he apparently hasn't learned his lesson, as he plans to find 'all the pretty girls' when he gets there.

'There's No Life Without Love' (Davies, Dave Davies)
B-side to 'Lincoln County'.

This is a simple love song with almost choral harmonies. We have the Nicky Hopkins harpsichord again, which cheers up an otherwise plodding song.

'Lazy Old Sun' (Stereo alternate take) (Davies)
This is a previously unreleased stereo take of the album track, recorded in June 1967.

Live At Kelvin Hall (1968)

Original UK label and catalogue number: Pye Records NPL18191 (Mono),
NSPL18191 (stereo)
Personnel:
Ray Davies: rhythm guitar, lead and backing vocals
Dave Davies: lead guitar, backing and lead vocals
Pete Quaife: bass, backing vocals
Mick Avory: drums,
Producer: Ray Davies
Running time: 34:18
Recorded at Kelvin Hall, Glasgow, 1 April 1967
Release dates: UK: 12 January 1968, US: 16 August 1967
Chart positions: UK: –, US: 162
Tracklist: 'Till The End Of The Day' (Davies), 'A Well Respected Man' (Davies),
'You're Looking Fine' (Davies), 'Sunny Afternoon' (Davies), 'Dandy' (Davies), 'I'm
On An Island' (Davies), 'Come On Now' (Davies), 'You Really Got Me' (Davies),
'Medley - Milk Cow Blues/Batman Theme /Tired Of Waiting For You/Milk Cow
Blues' (Estes, Hefti, Davies, Estes)

As previously mentioned, on 1 April 1967, the band and assorted engineers
drove up to Scotland and recorded the band's first live album. They performed
two shows on the night, one at 6:30 and the second at 9:30, with Sounds
Incorporated and The Fortunes opening the show. The recording – using the
Pye Mobile Recording Unit – was pretty basic. There was one microphone for
each guitar and Pete's bass, one for the bass drum and one for the rest of the
drum kit, two for vocals and one for the crowd. The crowd seems to win the
battle, though the album does give an accurate depiction of a Kinks gig in the
1960s: full of energy. Ray does manage to get control of the crowd, conducting
them in community singing of 'Sunny Afternoon' and 'Happy Birthday' –
although, with the crowd's screams, we can't hear why they sang it: the date
doesn't match any of the band's birthdays, so we can assume it's that of a
member of the audience. There were some overdubs made in post-production,
as the guitar solo on the stereo version of 'You Really Got Me' is different from
the mono version.

The sleeve was predominantly blue, with the title and a montage of
nine colour images from the show; the back cover having a tracklist and
a monochrome band shot. There weren't many live albums around in the
1960s, as recording technology for live shows was not that great and it was
brave of the band to release one. However, it sold poorly, and by the time it
was released in the UK, The Kinks had moved on, and it didn't really reflect
what they were about anyway: it's more of a retrospective. However, as a time
capsule, it's a good representation of the band at their live, sweaty best.

The Kinks Are The Village Green Preservation Society (1968)

Personnel:
Ray Davies: guitar, keyboards, harmonica, mellotron, lead vocals
Dave Davies: lead guitar, backing and lead vocals
Pete Quaife: bass, backing vocals
Mick Avory: drums, percussion
Additional personnel:
Rasa Davies: backing vocals
Nicky Hopkins: keyboards, mellotron
Producer: Ray Davies
Running time: 38:58
Recorded at Pye Studios, London (November 1966; Spring to October 1968)
Release dates: UK: 22 November 1968, US: January 1969
Original UK label and catalogue number: Pye Records NPL18233
Chart positions: UK: 47, US: –

Back in 1966, Ray had written a song about a mythical village green in which the old way of life still existed. He was lamenting the fact that this way of life was fast disappearing from the world in which he actually lived. As the band couldn't visit America, he decided to retreat into his native land – even dropping the faux American accent that most bands seemed to think they needed. This album could be regarded as Ray's magnum opus, as – 50 years on – it's now receiving the respect it deserves.

After the relative failure of *Something Else* and *Live At Kelvin Hall*, Ray thought the band would only have one more album in them, and he wanted to make a statement (In a way, he was correct, as this would be the last album the original lineup would make). Instead of singing about love and the hippy-trippy things that dominated the charts, Ray became more introspective and wrote about everyday things like family weddings, photograph albums, even cats. Both Ray and Dave – at 20 and 23, respectively – were saddened and angered by the changing way of life: thoughts more in keeping with people over twice their age.

According to Pete Quaife and Mick Avory, this was the most collaborative album the band made, with everyone contributing ideas. Again, the band didn't record the album in one go, but over a number of sessions, with the last two songs recorded just a month before release. But in the end, the overall vision was Ray's. Originally planned as a 12-track stereo album, the tapes were delivered to Pye, records pressed and even released in some countries, and there had even been a review in *New Musical Express*. But then Ray had second thoughts and wanted the album changed. The tracks 'Days' (a single in June 1968) and 'Mr. Songbird' were removed. Ray wanted more tracks added to make it a double album but to be sold for the price of a single album. Pye refused but compromised by making it a 15-track album. The additional tracks were 'Last Of The Steam-Powered Trains', 'Big Sky', Sitting By The Riverside', 'Animal Farm' and 'All Of My Friends Were There'.

The front cover was a treated image of the band, with the title and band name in red, the back cover being a band shot Barrie Wentzell took on Hampstead Heath, along with the lyrics to the opening track. The photos were not specifically taken for the album, and Barrie didn't know the images had been used until he bought a copy of the album.

The Kinks were definitely out of sync with the other hitmakers of the time. For instance, a line like 'Picture yourself when you're getting old' (from 'Picture Book') isn't what your typical record buyer wanted to do in 1968. But the failure of the album (which barely scraped into the UK top 50) was down to a number of reasons. Firstly, there were no apparent *hit* singles on it, and it was released on the same day as The Beatles' *White* album. Ray was proud of the album and was disappointed that it didn't sell – The Kinks were still considered a singles band, and he wanted to move on. Also, this would be the last original Kinks album to chart in their homeland. It eventually reached gold status in 2018.

It has long been debated whether *Village Green* was a concept album. I personally think that it is, and the record's importance cannot be overstated. Over the years, it became a standout and much-respected album, and Ray continued to write thematically for the next eight albums. It also led to him being approached by American band The Turtles, who wanted Ray to produce them, which he subsequently did.

The Village Green Preservation Society was a deeply personal album for Ray and not only looks to his past but is a Walt-Disney-like fantasy world into which he retreats.

'The Village Green Preservation Society' (Davies)
The opening track is probably the album's best-known. It's a statement of intent about preserving Ray's favourite things: cleverly listing them in rhyme. The final 'God save the village green' line became the battle cry for Kinks fans. In the music, we have some strong bass with guitar and keyboard joining in superbly. A change of key gives the end of the somg a bit more urgency.

'Do You Remember Walter?' (Davies)
This is about an old man remembering his old mate Walter and wondering if he ran into him now, would they still have things in common? Dave always felt sad playing this song, as he would remember friends he'd lost contact with. The underlying message is that people change, but the memories remain. The intro could've possibly inspired Jeff Lynne's intro to 'Mr. Blue Sky'.

'Picture Book' (Davies)
This lyric describes sitting by the fire looking at a family photo album. Ray lists all the types of photos we all have in our photograph albums. There is a slightly

different drum sound, as Mick took the snare off the snare drum to make it more thuddy. 'Picture Book' was an A-side in Australia and was the B-side to 'Starstruck' in America. In 2004, 'Picture Book' was used in a TV commercial for Hewlett-Packard digital imaging products.

'Johnny Thunder' (Davies)
Ray said this was based on a couple of Muswell Hill bikers he knew who were cool and always got the girls, and also on the Marlon Brando movie *The Wild One*. The character of Johnny Thunder was to return in the song 'One Of The Survivors' on The Kinks 1973 album *Preservation Act 1*. Dave Davies suggested that Pete Townshend of The Who was influenced by the song and used the opening riff of it on 'I Can't Explain', a song, Dave claimed, was meant to sound like The Kinks.

'Last Of The Steam-Powered Trains' (Davies)
This is a tribute to the US musicians who inspired Ray – especially Howlin' Wolf: this song has his 'Smokestack Lightning' all over it. It's a mid-tempo song after the preceding faster songs. The lyric is about Ray himself: one of the remaining few who adhered to the old ways. Sonically it's like a train chugging along the rails and slowly gets faster towards the end as it leaves the station.

'Big Sky' (Davies)
The main lyrics are spoken rather than sung: almost like a vicar preaching. It has been argued that it's about religion, and I would agree, but Ray has never given a definitive answer as to whether Big Sky is God. Seemingly 'Big Sky' is an allegory for an all-seeing power who just doesn't care about the little people 'like you and me' – but one day we will be free from its influence. It's one of Ray's favourite Kinks tracks, but he was unhappy with his performance of it.

'Sitting By The Riverside' (Davies)
Another of Ray's allegories. When he was about eight years old, he went fishing a lot, and this could be him looking back at that time. However, he could be using it as an allegory for just sitting back while life flows past. Nicky Hopkins' keyboards – mainly piano and accordion – fill out the song.

'Animal Farm' (Davies)
Another Ray Davies fantasy land (like his village green). Animal Farm is a place where we can all let ourselves go and play like the animals – after all, we're all animals anyway. This is a theme he would return to later, in 'Apeman' and 'Supersonic Rocket Ship'. There is a lot of reverb on the drums and the intro has piano. Pete thought that bass guitar should be included with the piano line in the intro, but both Ray and Dave said no. This song was the B-side to 'Village Green' in Japan.

'Village Green' (Davies)

Based on the Muswell Hill of his childhood, this was written and recorded in 1966/1967 and was the original inspiration for the album. A song about innocence and simpler times, it was also the fantasy land Ray would retreat to. Lyrically (and musically with woodwind and harpsichord), it's very English in outlook. George Orwell said that the 'air is different in England, and country life was freedom from the city'. Originally recorded for the *Something Else,* it was held back as Ray was collecting songs for the village green-themed album. It was released as an A-side in Japan. In the lyrics, the protagonist leaves the village to seek stardom and eventually misses his home. But the village has now become a tourist attraction.

'Starstruck' (Davies)

You want to seek fame and fortune, but you have to leave family and all that they stand for, behind; you've been 'taken in by the lights'. A lovely use of mellotron instead of strings gives this song a Moody Blues-type feel. It was a single in the US and Germany and reached 13 in The Netherlands.

'Phenomenal Cat' (Davies)

With its use of mellotron and flute, the intro would resurface on the track 'Lightning Strikes' on the 1999 Yes album *The Ladder*. It's a child's fantasy with Dave's voice sped up as the cat. This phenomenal cat has travelled the world and learned the meaning of life in Hong Kong. It's the album's most whimsical song.

'All Of My Friends Were There' (Davies)

Public embarrassment is the theme here. The performer becomes drunk before a big show and embarrasses himself. It was inspired by a real event when Ray had to perform with a temperature of 104. He'd had a lot to drink, and when the curtains opened, all his friends were in the front row. In the song, when the performer takes to the stage again, he is a big success.

'Wicked Annabella' (Davies)

A dark aura surrounds this song, which is almost heavy metal. Fuzz guitars and deep drums give this effect, and Mick is experimenting again by removing the snare. This is the only Dave lead vocal on the album. Wicked Annabella is a witch, and the track has a suitably-eerie ending. The Kinks never performed it live, but Dave does it at solo gigs.

'Monica' (Davies)

This is about a beautiful but aloof girl: probably the village prostitute. According to Ray, she was a real person – a modest girl he once danced with, but she looked down on men. There's a lovely calypso swing to this one.

'People Take Pictures Of Each Other' (Davies)

Ray's commentary about how people record their lives on camera is a fast number in the traditional music hall style. The stereo version (slated for the originally-scheduled 12-track album) has a big-band ending which, strangely, was edited from the final release.

Bonus Tracks from the 1998 reissue on Castle Communications (ESM CD 481)

A stereo version of the album with only 12 tracks (in a different order) rather than 15, was originally intended to be released on 27 September 1968. This stereo album was included as the bonus tracks.

'The Village Green Preservation Society' (Davies), 'Do You Remember Walter' (Davies), 'Picture Book' (Davies), 'Johnny Thunder' (Davies), 'Monica' (Davies), 'Days' (Davies) Stereo version of single, 'Village Green' (Davies)

'Mr. Songbird' (Davies)

A simple and happy little ditty about the joy of listening to the birds sing.

'Wicked Annabella' (Davies), 'Starstruck' (Davies), 'Phenomenal Cat' (Davies), 'People Take Pictures Of Each Other' (Davies)

'Days' (Mono single A-side version) (Davies)

UK release: Pye Records, 7N 17573, 28 June 1968. Producer: Ray Davies. Chart positions: UK: 12, US: –, Australia: 77

'Days' was recorded because Pye wanted a single on the *Village Green* album. But Ray wasn't happy about it, and it was eventually taken off the album before its release, though it was on the 12-track stereo version. It's one of Ray's more poignant songs – thinking about a former love and thanking them for the times they had together. The track was used in an advertisement for the Volkswagen Golf Cabriolet in 2011 and in *The Harry Hill Movie*. It reached 7 in the Netherlands and hit the top 20 in New Zealand and Belgium. Kirsty MacColl's version also got to 12 in Britain in 1989.

BMG/Sanctuary Records released a three-disc deluxe version of the album in 2004. The extra tracks from this release will be detailed in the 'Other Recordings Of Note' section.

Arthur Or The Decline And Fall Of The British Empire (1969)

Personnel:
Ray Davies: rhythm guitar, piano, harpsichord, lead and backing vocals
Dave Davies: lead guitar, backing and lead vocals
John Dalton: bass, backing vocals
Pete Quaife: bass, backing vocals (on bonus tracks)
Mick Avory: drums, percussion
John Gosling: keyboards
Producer: Ray Davies
String and horn arrangements: Lew Warburton
Running time: 49:17
Recorded at Pye Studios London (May/June 1969)
Release date: 10 October 1969
Original UK label and catalogue number: Pye Records NSPL18317
Chart positions: UK: –, US: 105

The Kinks' seventh studio album had a different birth from the previous six, as it was originally intended as the soundtrack of a television play. The band's management was approached by Granada TV producer Jo Durden-Smith, who wanted Ray to write a musical drama for their new colour service (Up until 1969, British television was broadcast in black and white). The only proviso was that Ray had to collaborate with a known writer. Ray suggested Alan Bennett and John Betjeman: the future poet laureate. The eventual collaborator was playwright and novelist Julian Mitchell, who had enjoyed critical success with his experimental novel *The Undiscovered Country*. The pair worked together well, and the screenplay and songs were completed quickly.

Ray based the story on his sister Rose and her husband Arthur's emigration to Australia. The title character was an everyman, going through emotional stress as he moved to the other side of the world. Also, there was added back story of the character's experiences in the war and commentary on the class system and the loss of the British Empire (The Empire became the Commonwealth in 1949).

Just before recording started, Ray travelled to Los Angeles to produce The Turtles' album *Turtle Soup* and also to negotiate an end to The Kinks US ban. The band also recorded Dave's solo album during the spring, but it was never released. It would be 1980 before we saw his first solo LP. Once the *Arthur* music had been recorded, the idea was to release the album in the autumn while it was being filmed; the part of Arthur being played by actor Frank Finlay. Then when the film was broadcast in January 1970, it boosted record sales. Sadly, the production was beset with delays and was eventually cancelled, but the album was released as planned.

This would be the last Kinks album to be released in mono in the UK, although it would be issued in stereo in the US. Three singles were taken from it – one in June, one in September just prior to the album release, and the other in December, whilst 'Plastic Man' was issued in March as a stopgap between releases. None of the singles managed to reach the top 30, and two failed to chart at all – something that befell the album, which didn't even make the top 100 in America, despite (or because of) being compared favourably to The Who's rock opera *Tommy,* which had been released earlier in the year.

The album cover – designed by Bob Lawrie – is a pretty dull affair. It's mainly brown, with the band name at the top. Underneath that are illustrations of Englishness – a teapot, a semidetached house, a swan, a photograph (of The Kinks) and a commemorative tea mug. The back cover had band portraits, a tracklist, an explanation of the plot (by Julian Mitchell), and notes by author and journalist Geoffrey Cannon outlining what The Kinks had been doing over the past five years.

A major change in The Kinks' world occurred at the beginning of the year with the final departure of Pete Quaife, who'd had enough of having his ideas dismissed by Ray and Dave. His replacement was the returning John Dalton, who was originally reluctant to return, but was eventually persuaded.

'Victoria' (Davies)

Released as a single A-side. UK release: Pye Records, 7N 17865, 12 December 1969. Producer: Ray Davies. Chart positions: UK: 33, US: 62, Australia: 57
This was the album's final single, and also the last Kinks release of the 1960s. A rock/blues guitar riff opens the song and continues throughout. There's a brass band in there too. It was a minor hit in Britain but very popular in Toronto for some reason, where it got to number nine in the local chart. In the *Arthur* story, Ray is satirising the Victorian era and the facts that her subjects weren't treated well and there was a massive gap between the rich and poor.

'Yes Sir, No Sir' (Davies)

This is about Arthur's experiences in the army. He has to follow orders all the time and is always being told what to do and when to do it. The song opens with a guitar and drum march, and the majority of the track has brass in the background.

'Some Mother's Son' (Davies)

A very effective and poignant anti-war song. A lot of soldiers are little more than children. The 'son' in the song looks up at the sun, and is shot dead and lies in the field. All that the family has left of him is his picture in a frame at home. The wailing chorus signifies the sadness and hopelessness of the lyric.

'Drivin'' (Davies)

The first single taken from the album. UK release: Pye Records, 7N 17776, 20 June 1969
Producer: Ray Davies. Chart positions: Did not chart
The album's first single. The rhythm conjures up the image of a drive in the country. It could've been inspired by Ray's father taking the family out in the car into the country. In the story, Arthur takes his wife for a drive to forget problems, but it's only a brief respite.

'Brainwashed' (Davies)

There's some brass and very loud guitar on this rocker which was released as the B-side to 'Victoria' in America. Ray is telling us that the population has been brainwashed into knowing their place in society – another of Ray's digs at the class system.

'Australia' (Davies)

Dave sings a co-lead vocal on this. It was released as an A-side in Australia but didn't chart. Arthur's son Derek is trying to convince him of the opportunities in Australia ('no drug addiction'). The part where he tells of being able to 'surf like they do in the USA' has Ray cheekily adding some Beach-Boys-like vocal harmonies. The middle section has a lengthy jam (presumably, the TV show would've shown images of Australia) and even features the wobble board, but you have to listen hard to hear it.

'Shangri-La' (Davies)

The album's second single. UK release: Pye Records, 7N 17812, 12 September 1969. Producer: Ray Davies. Chart positions: Did not chart
'Shangrila' is another swipe at the class system. Ray based this on his sister's house in Adelaide. The hard rock denotes Arthur's anger that his new lifestyle in Australia isn't how he imagined. It was not a successful single, although it reached 27 in the Netherlands. This is John Dalton's favourite Kinks song. Arthur is reflecting that his house has been paid for by his hard work.

'Mr. Churchill Says' (Davies)

B-side to 'Victoria in the UK.
On 'Mr. Churchill Says', some of Winston Churchill's most famous utterances are paraphrased, and other famous people of the time are mentioned. There is the sound of an air-raid siren. A highlight of the track is a trippy section with guitar and chanting. Another reminiscence about the war.

'She's Bought A Hat Like Princess Marina' (Davies)

B-side to 'Australia' in Australia. It's yet another dig at the class system (Ray really had a bee in his bonnet about class) – you can buy classy clothes and be a bit snobby, but you can't afford food; you're getting your priorities wrong; don't think above your station in life. 'She has a hat like Princess Marina' and 'He has a hat like Anthony Eden'. And they don't care. It's keyboard-led with piano and harpsichord to the fore.

'Young And Innocent Days' (Davies)
Arthur is being nostalgic for the past, when things were simpler – shades of the village green here. He is probably homesick. It's a poignant song with lots of acoustic guitar to give it a reflective vibe.

'Nothing To Say' (Davies)
A sad, almost bluesy song about when families drift apart. Musically, everything is in this one – blues, brass, choir, heavy metal guitar, you name it.

'Arthur' (Davies)
Dave sings co-lead vocal again here. In the beginning, Arthur was young and ambitious, but the world has passed him by. He's been right all along and shouldn't have moved. Life is good in England, so why emigrate to the other side of the world? There is some good country guitar on this track, which ends up quite jolly.

Bonus Tracks from the 1998 reissue on Castle Communications (ESM CD 511)
'Plastic Man' (Mono single version) (Davies)
Single A-side. UK release: Pye Records, 7N 17724, 28 March 1969. Producer: Ray Davies. Chart positions: UK: 31, US: –, Australia: 97
The A-side was a deliberate attempt at a hit single, recorded and released in March 1969. Pete Quaife hated it, although he supplied the falsetto vocal just before leaving the band (Could this song have been the last straw?). The BBC refused to play it, as it had the word 'bum', which effectively scuppered its chances of being a bigger hit. Ray says it's about everything becoming a commodity. It's one of my personal favourites.

'King Kong' (Mono) (Davies)
B-side to 'Plastic Man'.
'King Kong' is a heavy blues song and a veiled attack on the music publisher Edward Kassner. Ray had a long-running dispute with him over the songs, and this could be a precursor to Ray's attack on the music industry that would come on the next album. Pete was still in the band, as it was recorded during the same session as 'Plastic Man'.

'Drivin'' (Mono single version) (Davies)

'Mindless Child Of Motherhood' (Mono) (Dave Davies)

B-side to 'Drivin''.

On the B-side, Dave shares his pain and anger about being parted from the girl he got pregnant at school, resulting in his being expelled. The softer sections are him reminiscing about the girl, and the harder sections are expressions of anger.

'This Man He Weeps Tonight' (Mono) (Dave Davies)

B-side of 'Shangri-La'.

On this B-side, Dave sings lead vocal on his own song, which was originally meant for his solo album. Pete Quaife is still in the fold here. The subject of the song is alone and feeling sorry for himself.

'Plastic Man' (Stereo mix) (Davies), 'Mindless Child Of Motherhood' (Stereo mix) (Dave Davies), 'This Man He Weeps Tonight' (Stereo mix) (Dave Davies), 'She's Bought A Hat Like Princess Marina' (Mono take) (Davies)

'Mr. Shoemaker's Daughter' (Stereo) (Dave Davies)

Dave is saying to all the girls of the town – the daughters of the shoemaker, cake baker, bread baker and greengrocer – that he's coming home. In other words, 'Lock up your daughters!'. It sounds very much like a Bob Dylan track.

Lola Versus Powerman And The Moneygoround, Part One (1970)

Personnel:
Ray Davies: resonator guitar, guitar, keyboards, harmonica, lead vocals
Dave Davies: lead guitar, banjo, backing and lead vocals
John Dalton: bass, backing vocals
John Gosling: keyboards, piano, organ
Mick Avory: drums, tambourine
Producer: Ray Davies
Running time: 40:25
Recorded at Morgan Studios, Willesden, London (April, May, August and September 1970)
Release dates: 27 November 1970
Original UK label and catalogue number: Pye Records NSPL18359
Chart positions: UK: −, US: 35, Australia: 24

The Kinks entered the 1970s determined to win back their popularity in America. They had played around 20 dates in the States between October and Christmas 1969, and found that touring had changed. Gone were the package tours; the audiences had matured and wanted more of an *event*. The band were well-received and hailed as cult heroes. Their American record company Reprise saw fit to issue an 18-track compilation titled *God Save The Kinks*, to let the people know what had gone before.

But things never go smoothly with this band, and when they returned to the US for another tour in January 1970, Mick Avory came down with hepatitis, and the tour was cancelled after just four shows… but they would be back soon. While Mick recovered, Ray appeared in 'The Long Distance Piano Player': part of the BBC's *Play For Today* series. In it, he played a Yorkshireman about to take part in a marathon piano-playing contest. The play was broadcast on 15 October, and Ray, in particular, received good reviews.

Armed with a new batch of songs, The Kinks started recording their first album of the new decade at Morgan Studios in Willesden. Ray had been dissatisfied with the sound quality at Pye Studios for some time, and especially during the recording of 'Plastic Man'. So after a try-out, he decided to record at Morgan.

The band had a new member in the form of John 'The Baptist' Gosling. Most of the previous singles and albums included keyboards, and it was Grenville Collins who suggested the band could benefit from the augmentation of a permanent keyboard player, more particularly for live work where the sound needed filling out. John had been playing church organ in Stoke Newington when he answered the advert in *ZigZag* magazine and was nicknamed 'John The Baptist' as he had a long beard and a big duffel coat with a hood. John was born in Paignton, Devon, on 6 February 1948, and one of his earlier bands –

The Challengers – were inspired to play after hearing The Kinks' record 'Long Tall Sally' on the radio. After a successful audition – during which the band laid down some backing tracks for the new album – John was invited to join in May and made his live debut with the band on 22 May in Minneapolis, after having filmed a promo for the new single 'Lola'.

1970 was also the year The Kinks recorded two albums. The second was recorded in October and would be released early in 1972. This was the soundtrack to the film *Percy*, but more about that later. The main event for the year was the album *Lola Versus Powerman And The Moneygoround, Part One*, which would be Ray's swipe at the music industry. Yes, in a way, he was biting the hand that fed him, but he'd had enough of the politics and machinations of the music biz. On the album, nobody escapes from Ray's scrutiny – publishers, unions, the press, accountants, management and touring are all put under the Davies microscope. Two singles were released from the album – 'Lola' in June and 'Apeman' in November – both of which charted, with 'Lola' being their biggest hit for three years, and their final top ten single.

The album had a monochrome cover. On the back was a depiction of Leonardo Da Vinci's Vitruvian Man surrounded by concentric circles and squares, plus a tracklist). The front was basically the same, but with 'Kinks' in blue script and the album title in black script. A face with quarters of the four main band members replaced the Vitruvian Man – top left, Dave; top right, Mick; bottom left, John Dalton; bottom right, Ray. John Gosling was not represented.

The album was lauded by the music press in both Britain and America, with *Rolling Stone* calling it 'the best Kinks album yet'. *New Musical Express* praised the album's originality, calling Ray Davies 'one of the finest writers in contemporary rock'. Despite this praise and the hit singles which preceded the album's release, it sold poorly. A *Part Two* was planned but ultimately scrapped in favour of *Muswell Hillbillies*. Aside from *Percy*, the next six albums would see The Kinks embrace the idea of *concept* albums and make their live shows into theatrical events.

The good thing about the two hits was they enabled the band to negotiate a new contract with RCA Records when their Pye contract ended.

'The Contender' (Davies)
This starts with a gentle country-style intro before erupting into an out-and-out hard-rocking number. Piano is to the fore with Ray's bluesy harmonica. It's the start of our young hopeful's journey in the corrupt music industry.

It was inspired in part by the I could've been a contender' line in the film *On The Waterfront* and a DJ introducing The Kinks as a contender for the top spot in the charts.

'Strangers' (Dave Davies)
An acoustic-led song with guitar, piano, organ and vibes giving a relaxed feel. The message is that we're better off united than divided – 'We are not two, we

are one'. This is one of two Dave Davies compositions on the album, and he says 'Strangers' was partly inspired by an old school friend who died from a drug overdose. There is superb singing from Dave and great, thudding drums in the outro.

'Denmark Street' (Davies)

This is the album's first swipe at the industry, and the target is the music publishers (They were mainly based on Denmark Street). Our hero is trying to get his song published, but the publisher doesn't like him or the song but signs him up anyway, as 'He doesn't like to be wrong'. This is a barrelhouse song, very much in the music hall vein.

'Get Back In The Line' (Davies)

This ballad is about Ray's view of the unions and working-class struggles. Again, it's inspired by the film *On The Waterfront* – in particular the last scene where the hero is beaten up and told to get back in the work line. It was also influenced by Ray seeing his father in a dole queue.

'Lola' (Davies)

UK release: Pye Records, 7N 17961, 12 June 1970, Producer: Ray Davies, Chart positions: UK: 2, US: 9, Australia: 4

This is the last Kinks single to get into the top ten in the UK, reaching two, although some charts put it at one. It topped the charts in Ireland, the Netherlands and New Zealand, and was a top-five hit in Germany and Canada. Ray wanted the intro to stand out, and on a shopping trip to Shaftesbury Avenue in London, he bought a 1938 National Steel Resonator guitar for £150 and played the intro on it: doubled with a Martin guitar.

The story behind the song is often told, and like The Hollies' 'Stop Stop Stop', takes place in a nightclub. Apparently, manager Robert Wace was dancing in a Paris nightclub with a beautiful woman, but at the end of the night, failed to notice the five-o'clock stubble. The BBC was not going to play the song, as they objected to the use of the brand name Coca Cola, so Ray – who was in America at the time – flew a 6000-mile round trip to change 'Coca Cola' to 'cherry cola'. It seems strange today that the Beeb would object to a brand name yet happily play a song about a transvestite!

'Top Of The Pops' (Davies)

With a spoken intro by Dave Symms, Ray has a go at the press and hit-making machine and what artists have to do to get promotion. But at least at the end of the song, our hero is at number 1. The spoken intro is almost a copy of the intro to the influential BBC TV show of the title, and Ray sets the scene by having the song sound reminiscent of The Kinks' early hits and other hits of the time (Listen closely).

'The Moneygoround' (Davies)

Accountants and managers are on the receiving end of Ray's barbed tongue here. He actually name-checks the band's management team of Grenville Collins, Robert Wace and Larry Page. He is wondering where all the money has gone, and it goes ''round and 'round' without him getting his rightful share. He does get his money, but only after everybody else has taken their share. This was Ray's take on the legal publishing wrangles over the past few years. It caused a rift between him and the managers, and within a year, they had parted company. Musically, it appears to be a happy little ditty in the music hall style. But underneath, the lyrics are sardonic and biting.

'This Time Tomorrow' (Davies)

The Kinks had been touring pretty much all the time since 1964. Every touring band enter their own touring bubble, and it's a monotonous slog at times, especially when you're losing touch with your family. The singer is in an aeroplane, wondering where he'll be tomorrow, and he starts fantasising about the places he could be.

The song has been described as a melancholy ballad, and Ray again uses the Resonator guitar that he used on 'Lola' (See the notes on 'Lola'). The sound effect of an aeroplane taking off sets the scene.

'A Long Way From Home' (Davies)

In the liner notes to the 2020 album reissue, Ray says this ballad is a gentle warning to Dave to not forget your roots. Gentle guitar and keyboard lead into an almost pleading vocal from Ray.

'Rats' (Dave Davies)

B-side to 'Apeman'.

This is about the *suits* of the music industry. Dave's inspiration came from when he was looking for a job and the experience of being talked down to. The B-side is the second Dave Davies track on the album, and as Ray took a firmer hold on the reins, Dave would not contribute another song to an album until the next decade. Dave sings lead vocals on this hard rock number and supplies some heavy guitar work.

'Apeman' (Davies)

UK release: Pye Records, 7N 45016, 20 November 1970, Producer: Ray Davies, Chart positions: UK: 5, US: 45, Australia: 5

This was a top-five hit in Germany and New Zealand, top ten in Ireland and the Netherlands, and top-20 in Canada. It's a nifty piece of faux calypso, and the sound effects include Dave's E-type Jaguar. Again, Ray had to fly back and re-record a single word. The lyrics state, 'The air pollution is a-fogging up my eyes'. However, 'fogging' sounded like another word beginning with f, so it had to be redone. Ray said at the time, 'My diction is terrible'.

Man is the cause of all problems, and our hero is fed up with the modern world. He wants to 'sail away to a distant shore'. The lyric dabbles a bit in nostalgia, similar in vein to *The Village Green Preservation Society.*

'Powerman' (Davies)

In this hard rock song, Powerman represents the power behind the industry executives. Our hero is at the end of his tether, as no matter what he does, Powerman has him 'in the palm of his hand'. Ray introduces a cheeky line about how his girl really got him going, which is a nod to the first hit. Ray and Dave share lead vocals on this song.

'Got To Be Free' (Davies)

Ray wrote this for the BBC *Play For Today* 'The Long Distance Piano Player', and adapted it for use on the album. It starts as a kind of lullaby before heading into mainstream rock. Ray again uses the Resonator guitar to good effect, and it's teamed up with a banjo. There is a slight country feel, which would be carried over to The Kinks' next concept *Muswell Hillbillies*. Lyrically, it's the finale to the story, with our hero longing for a better world as he vows to fight the system and live the life he chooses.

Bonus Tracks from the 1998 reissue on Castle Communications (ESM CD 509)

'Lola' (Mono single mix) (Davies)

The version that was released as a single in the UK.

'Apeman' (Demo) (Davies)

The demo version of the album's second single. In fact, it was this version that was issued as an A-side in Denmark.

'Powerman' (Demo) (Davies)

A previously unreleased mix of the album track, according to the reissue notes. To be honest, this is wrong, as a 'demo' is not an alternative mix of a song; it's a totally different recording.

The 2020 album reissue released by BMG (BMGCAT434DCD) has some other interesting alternate mixes and tracks – an instrumental version of 'The Contenders', live versions of 'Get Back In Line' and 'A Long Way From Home', and a version of 'Lola' recorded by Ray Davies and his band, which featured keyboardist Ian Gibbons (see later) with The Danish National Chamber Orchestra and The Danish National Vocal Ensemble recorded in 2010.

The following tracks were not on the original album but were recorded for possible inclusion:

'Anytime' (Davies)
This is similar in theme to 'Strangers', and that's probably why it was eventually left off. This is an affirmation of friendship. 'Anytime you're down, I'll be there'.

'The Good Life' (Davies)
A blues number that has our hero being seduced by the industry's darker side. All he can do is 'put his body around', says the man with the Havana cigar; then you'll have the good life.

'Marathon' (Davies)
The first of two songs here that were originally heard on the BBC *Play For Today* 'The Long Distance Piano Player'. Vocals by Ray Davies; piano by Fiachra Trench.

'Got To Be Free' (Davies)
This is the original version of the song on the album, edited from the BBC show. Vocals by Ray Davies; piano by Fiachra Trench.

Percy – Original Soundtrack (1971)

Personnel:
Ray Davies: acoustic guitars, harmonica, vocals
Dave Davies: 6 and 12-string electric guitars, vocals
John Dalton: bass, lead and backing vocals
Mick Avory: drums
John Gosling: keyboards
Additional personnel:
Rick Wakeman: piano, organ, harpsichord (Film version)
Stanley Myers: orchestral arrangements
Producer: Ray Davies
Running time: 33:03
Recorded at Morgan Studios, Willesden, London (October 1970)
Release dates: 26 March 1971 (Not released in the US)
Original UK label and catalogue number: Pye Records NSPL18365
Chart positions: Did not chart

While working on *Lola Versus Powerman And The Moneygoround,* the band
worked on the soundtrack of the film *Percy.* It starred Hywel Bennett as Edwin
Anthony – the recipient (following an accident) of the world's first penis
transplant. It was based on the book by Raymond Hitchcock (no, really) and
was made by Anglo EMI, produced by Betty Box and directed by Ralph Thomas
– so it was almost a *Carry On* film. After the transplant, Edwin sets off to find
the identity of Percy's previous owner and somehow manages to work his way
around some of the donor's ex-girlfriends, such as Elke Sommer, Britt Ekland,
Adrienne Posta and others. It also features a cameo from footballer George Best.
The budget was £300,000, and the film eventually made a profit of £500,000.
Percy had its premier at Shaftesbury Avenue, London, on 11 February 1971 and
was the eighth-most-popular film at the British box office that year.

Importantly for The Kinks, this album was the last under their Pye contract,
and they were free to sign with a new record company, which would turn out
to be RCA. In the meantime, *Percy* was released a month after the film was
premiered and contained some of Ray's most touching songs, which seemed to
be ignored, as the album sold poorly, as did the EP released in April 1971. No
singles were released from the album in the UK. It was never released in the
US, but two tracks – 'God's Children' and 'Willesden Green' – appeared on the
compilation *The Kink Kronikles*, whilst 'The Way Love Used To Be' appeared on
the US compilation *The Great Lost Kinks Album.*

The cover is in orange and yellow and features the torso of a man with a
strategically-placed green fig leaf, along with the band's name, album title,
and film info in black. It was based on the artwork for the film posters by
John Troke.

Percy was Ray's second foray into film music, as he'd previously written the
march for the film *The Virgin Soldiers* (which, coincidentally, also starred Hywel

Bennett). It was a learning curve for Ray, as he explained, 'I spent all my time with a stopwatch, matching the music to the footage'. He had to record it all twice, once for the album and again for the music that's actually heard on the film.

Although not credited on the album, keyboardist Rick Wakeman also played on the soundtrack, as he explained to me: 'The score for the film was composed – based on 'Lola' mainly – by Stanley Myers, and it was recorded at Olympic Studios in Barnes. I played piano, organ and harpsichord. It was with a full orchestra, and everything was recorded on the same day'.

'God's Children' (Davies)
A gentle, piano-based song which serves as the film's main theme. Lyrically and thematically, it's another version of 'Apeman', with the protagonist wanting to go back to the way God made us. In a way, he's rejecting scientific progress, which in effect, is the premise of the film. Without progress, he wouldn't have Percy.

This was released as a single in the US but failed to chart. It did, however, reach 53 in Australia and 21 in New Zealand.

'Lola' (Instrumental) (Davies)
An instrumental version of the hit which was apparently the basis for the orchestral arrangements. This version, though, is perhaps a little long. Easy listening meets heavy rock.

'The Way Love Used To Be' (Davies)
This features lush strings with acoustic guitar and piano. Ray appears to be warning us against sexual promiscuity and wants to go back to a more romantic time. He was quite precognitive here, considering what would happen in ten years time with the AIDS epidemic.

'Completely' (Instrumental) (Davies)
A blues shuffle. All film soundtracks seem to have a recurring musical motif throughout, and this one has hints of 'Lola'. As Rick Wakeman said, a great deal of Stanley Myers' orchestration was based on the song. It has a very sudden end.

'Running Round Town' (Instrumental) (Davies)
This does give the impression of rushing around – almost like a train, and then it slows down as though we've reached our destination. There's some great Ray Davies harmonica on this song.

'Moments' (Davies)
A nostalgic and slow song, wanting to remember the good things: 'moments of ecstatic happiness'. He doesn't want to let the world get him down.

'Animals In The Zoo' (Davies)
This funky song is the most upbeat on the album, but lyrically it's another anti-progress song in the style of 'Apeman' and 'God's Children'. This would've been a better bet for a single release, as it's catchier.

'Just Friends' (Davies)
This sounds like a music box at the start, and the protagonist says he wants to be friends and nothing else. Ray performs a fine mock-1920s crooner style for the bridge, and the song ends with the orchestra and harpsichord.

'Whip Lady' (Instrumental) (Davies)
There's a deceptively gentle start with soft, tinkling piano, before the hard drums and guitar come in with shades of 'Acid Queen' from The Who's rock opera, *Tommy*.

'Dreams' (Davies)
Another soft and gentle start preceding a rock song, where our hero wonders what he would be if he lived in his dreams. It's one of Ray's fantasy songs, where he's looking for an escape from his ordinary life.

'Helga' (Instrumental) (Davies)
You can't escape the Latin flavour in this song. But in the film, Helga is played by Elke Sommer: a Scandinavian beauty. Ray supplies some scat vocals over some stylish flamenco guitar.

'Willesden Green' (Davies)
This mock-country song is the only one here where neither Ray nor Dave sing the lead vocal. It's John Dalton doing his Elvis impersonation. John was quite pleased about singing it, as he explains: 'I think it was being played when they went in a pub, so in a way, I was a pub singer. It was quite an honour that Ray and Dave let someone else sing a song'.

'God's Children (End)' (Instrumental) (Davies)
A reprise of the opening song.

Bonus Tracks from the 1998 reissue on Castle Communications (ESM CD 509)
'Dreams' (Film version in mono) (Davies)
'Moments' (Film version in mono) (Davies)
'The Way Love Used To Be' (Film version in mono) (Davies)
'The Way Love Used To Be' (Film version in mono) (Davies)
'The Way Love Used To Be' (Film version in mono) (Davies)

Five mono tracks that were heard in the actual film rather than on the soundtrack album. The three versions of 'The Way Used To Be' are all different. The first is an orchestral instrumental, while the second is again orchestral but with a vocal from Ray. The third has a 'seventies' vibe with organ and a jazzy bass and drum rhythm.

Muswell Hillbillies (1971)

Personnel:
Ray Davies: acoustic guitar, resonator guitar, lead vocals
Dave Davies: lead guitar, slide guitar, banjo, backing vocals
John Dalton: bass, backing vocals
Mick Avory: drums, percussion
John Gosling: acoustic and electric piano, Hammond organ, accordion
Additional personnel:
Mike Cotton: trumpet
John Beecham: trombone, tuba
Alan Holmes: saxophone, clarinet
Vicki Brown: backing vocals
Ken Jones: harmonica
Producer: Raymond Douglas Davies
Running time: 44:38
Recorded at Morgan Studios, Willesden, London (August-October 1971)
Release dates: UK: 26 November 1971, US: 24 November 1971
Original UK label and catalogue number: RCA Victor Records SF 8243
Chart positions: UK: –, US: 48, Australia: 36

With *Percy* completing their commitments to Pye, The Kinks were 'for sale' and interest was high. Ray and the management were being courted, but it would be the end of 1971 before the band signed to a new label. In the meantime, they undertook tours of the UK, US and Australia. The American and Australian dates were well received but were dogged by bad luck, equipment failures and health concerns over Dave Davies. He was admitted to hospital twice during the year, suffering from depression. The band was also partying hard, which didn't help.

In August, they entered Morgan Studios to start recording their new album. The recording process was a happy one, as they were quite close to Dave's home, and the two brothers would often carry on working there after the sessions had ceased for the day. The family would also visit the local pub: the Archway Tavern at the bottom of Highgate Hill. The atmosphere there, with live music, was so good that the photographs for the new album cover were taken there.

The two Johns – Dalton and Gosling – had more input into this album, frequently coming up with intros and sections that were approved by Ray, who by now knew exactly what he wanted and was in complete control of the band. John Gosling, in particular, has a strong showing on the album, even playing the accordion – he had tour manager Ken Jones pumping the instrument while John concentrated on his fingering.

The concept for the new album was Ray's fear of the upheaval of working-class people from their old homes into newer buildings. It was again revisiting themes from *The Village Green Preservation Society*. But where that album was pining for what we were losing, the new album would be distrust and disdain for what was replacing it. It was a theme close to Ray's heart, as his own family had been forced to relocate from their old family home in the Islington/King's Cross area to Muswell Hill. It was a move of only about five miles, but to these working-class people it was a whole new world. Ray likened it to the American TV show *The Beverly Hillbillies*, where the Clampett family struck oil, loaded everything onto their truck and moved to a mansion in Beverly Hills: hence *Muswell Hillbillies*.

Sonically, Ray gets a country rock feel for the album to fit in with the hillbilly theme, and therefore, it's a mix of his London roots and love of Americana. In the studio, The Mike Cotton Sound joined The Kinks for two tracks. This attempt at getting a fuller sound proved to be so successful that The Mike Cotton Sound were used in the live shows and on the next five albums.

Overall, the album has a retro sound in order to give a nostalgic feel. Ray achieved this by deliberately using dated recording techniques. However, he used modern equipment on '20th Century Man'. One of his innovations was to give the horn section a sound more akin to the 1920s or 1930s by having them record in a separate room to the microphone – in actual fact, some of the overdubs were done in the toilet at Morgan Studios.

During the summer of 1971, negotiations were still in progress for a new record company. It was agreed they needed a label with more international clout than Pye, as The Kinks were concentrating on rebuilding their reputation in America, and RCA seemed the best option. Ray cheekily asked Robert Wace to ask for another £100,000 on top of the offer already made, and they got it. The deal was very important for the band's future, as the advance was big enough for them to purchase an old derelict factory in Hornsea, North London, which they converted into their own studio, named Konk Studio. The band signed to RCA early in November 1971 for $1,000,000. The deal was to provide five albums (they did six), and *Muswell Hillbillies* was released at the end of that month.

The album cover – a gatefold sleeve designed by the Bloomsbury Group – featured the band at the bar of the Archway Tavern, and the inside showed them against a corrugated iron fence surrounding buildings that were due for demolition. Another photo showed them at a road sign pointing the way to Muswell Hill, Hornsea and Holloway: all within a couple of miles of each other.

Having grown frustrated with Pye Records' emphasis on hit singles, Ray deliberately decided to not include an obvious single on the album, preferring to keep his vision intact: consequently, no singles were issued in the UK. The critics loved the album, hailing it as one of Ray's best works, but their enthusiasm wasn't shared by the record-buying public. The album failed to chart in the UK and barely scraped into the top 50 in America.

The deal with RCA was the last management function that Wace and Collins had a hand in. Collins left first, and Wace soon after; their management contract terminated on 30 December 1971. Ray Davies took over management duties, thereby having overall control of the band. He could do whatever he wanted.

'20th Century Man' (Davies)

Ray sets the scene for the whole album. He is a modern man, but life is 'a mechanical nightmare'. The song starts very softly before building into an acceptable rocker. It had a more modern sound than the rest of the album, as more up-to-date recording equipment was used, in part making it one of the album's more radio-friendly songs, despite it being almost six minutes long. A single version – two minutes shorter – was released in the US, where it only reached 106 in the *Billboard* chart. The lyric tells us what Ray thinks about poverty and housing development, and it's apparent that he's against it.

'Acute Schizophrenia Paranoia Blues' (Davies)

This song is about the feeling that everyone is watching you in this technological age. Perhaps Ray had been reading *1984*. The darker aspect of this track is softened by the brass section and the overall feel which recalls both jazz and blues.

'Holiday' (Davies)

Perhaps a holiday will help: actually, no. We are revisiting 'Holiday On Waikiki' from the album *Face To Face.* There's no sun, and the sea is polluted. But in traditional British working-class style, the singer is determined to make the best of it. This is one of Ray's music hall songs, with honky-tonk piano and accordion.

'Skin And Bone' (Davies)

B-side to the single '20th Century Man' in the US. This is Ray's attack on the fad diets that were becoming popular at the time. It was a blues shuffle with a country feel, but when played live it was more of a rock song.

'Alcohol' (Davies)

Ray's tirade against the 'demon alcohol'. He had possibly seen what it was doing to Dave, but then Ray would end up having his own problems with it. This song, along with 'Skin And Bone', was a staple of the live set for many years and features the brass section to great effect – perhaps Ray was aiming for a sound like a Salvation Army temperance band.

'Complicated Life' (Davies)

A song about the stresses of everyday life, viewed from the eye of Ray Davies. There is slide guitar, giving the song the country-rock sound that Ray wanted, but it was countered with the jazz played by the brass section.

'Here Come The People In Grey' (Davies)
In this song, 'the people in grey' are the faceless bureaucrats who decide about such things as compulsory purchase and making people relocate. There's some great fuzz guitar from Dave, giving the song a more rock and roll sound, although the country blues sound still dominates: as it does the whole album.

'Have A Cuppa Tea' (Davies)
This is based on Ray and Dave's grandmother, who they loved visiting for her wisdom and stories. It's a British tradition and belief that a cup of tea makes everything alright. Ray based some of the lyrics on 'Sugartime': a 1958 hit for the McGuire Sisters. Quite a jolly song, and the album's happiest, it actually sounds like a sing-song around the piano.

'Holloway Jail' (Davies)
As with many of his songs, Ray based this song on a female he knew – someone successful in the city who was lured into crime and ended up in jail. It's sung from the point of view of the partner of the lady in question. It's a very bluesy song.

'Oklahoma U.S.A.' (Davies)
Another fantasy song. The girl in the song is tired of her monotonous life, and imagines herself in Oklahoma. Ray even mentions 'the surrey with the fringe on top', which is a song from the musical *Oklahoma*. A bit of name-dropping, too, as she dreams of being with stars like Shirley Jones and Gordon McRae (the stars of the film) and fantasizes that she is Rita Hayworth or Doris Day and that Errol Flynn will "take her away". It's a quieter song with no drums, just acoustic guitar, accordion, piano and organ.

'Uncle Son' (Davies)
Uncle Son is a working man under pressure from the unions and politicians using 'words he didn't understand' to get him to do what they want. It's the album's shortest song at just two and a half minutes. The uncle's despair comes across in the arrangement, which has a 'Gospel' feel accentuated by the organ and a bluesy slide guitar

'Muswell Hillbilly' (Davies)
This was based on the Davies family being forced to move to Muswell Hill. Ray likens it to the hillbillies of America and refers to places like West Virginia and New Orleans, although he admits he's never been. The character in the song – Rosie Rooke – was a childhood friend of Ray's mum. It's full of ironic lyrics and has a great country sound. He sings of saying goodbye to his girl and her 'bloodshot alcoholic eyes' and dreaming 'of the Black Hills that I ain't ever seen'. It would possibly have been a sizeable hit if it had been

released as a single. It was released as a single in Japan, with 'Oklahoma U.S.A.' on the flip side.

Bonus Tracks from the 1998 reissue on Konk/Velvel (63467-79719-2)
'Mountain Woman' (Davies)
This song – recorded in September 1971 during the album sessions – also has a country feel, in keeping with the rest of the set, but was eventually left off. After all, the album was already The Kinks' third-longest. The woman in the song is uneducated but happy. Then they are forcibly moved to a high-rise, and she now has all the creature comforts while they have built a dam on the site of her old house – yet she is still happy and making the most of things.

'Kentucky Moon' (Demo) (Davies)
Recorded on the same day as 'Mountain Woman' but left unfinished, this is yet another fantasy song. The singer only knows about Kentucky from the TV and tries to imagine living there. It's Ray singing over basic guitar, piano, organ and drums.

Everybody's In Show-biz (1972)

Personnel:
Ray Davies: acoustic guitar, resonator guitar, lead vocals
Dave Davies: lead guitar, slide guitar, banjo, 12-string acoustic, backing and lead vocals
John Dalton: bass, backing vocals
Mick Avory: drums
John Gosling: keyboards
Additional personnel:
Mike Cotton: trumpet
John Beecham: trombone, tuba
Alan Holmes: saxophone, clarinet (Studio recordings)
Dave Rowberry: organ ('Celluloid Heroes')
Davy Jones: baritone saxophone, clarinet (Live recordings)
Producer: Raymond Douglas Davies
Running time: 69:26
Recorded at Morgan Studios, Willesden, London (March-June 1972)
Live tracks recorded at Carnegie Hall, New York City (2/3 March 1972)
Release dates: UK: 1 September 1972, US: 25 August 1972
Original UK label and catalogue number: RCA Victor Records DPS2035
Chart positions: UK: –, US: 111, Australia: 38

The Kinks were now rapidly regaining their popularity in America, and Ray was becoming more and more of a frontman. Gone was the shy, slightly reluctant singer, and in its place was a showman: energetic and very much *in your face*. The audience still demanded the hits, and the band – even though Ray wanted to head in different directions – always played a selection of them in the live shows, sometimes in medley formats. However, Ray had new music to showcase, and the shows were about to become more theatrical. He augmented the stage lineup with The Mike Cotton Sound to help give the fuller sound he was getting on record. Dave wasn't a fan at first, as he was sometimes playing the same notes, and his guitar was getting lost in the mix.

One of the first recordings of the new lineup was a concert filmed at the Rainbow Theatre for the BBC. Although it was filmed in January 1972, it wasn't broadcast until July (See *The Kinks At The BBC* in the Other Releases Of Note section). Ray's original idea was an event centred on the albums *Village Green Preservation Society, Arthur* and *Muswell Hillbillies*. But the set they played was mainly hits, with just a couple of new songs, although there was some music from the *Virgin Soldiers* film. Perhaps the rock-band/horn-section fusion wasn't quite ready.

As part of the relaunch process, the band travelled to America at the end of February for a tour (the first of three that year), and by all accounts, it was the smoothest tour so far – there was no trouble, and the audiences greeted the band with enthusiasm. The two shows at New York's Carnegie Hall on 2 and

3 March 1972 were recorded. 11 of the songs from 3 March would end up on the band's next album (more about which in a little while), and more would appear on reissues in 1998 and 2016. In 1972, for the first time, The Kinks released a double album – one disc of new studio material, and the second was a live album containing songs recorded at Carnegie Hall.

Over several sessions between March and June, the band recorded the new material in Morgan Studios (The band's own studio wasn't ready), and *Everybody's In Showbiz* was released in the US in August and the UK a week later. Two singles were released from it in Britain and America: 'Supersonic Rocket Ship' and 'Celluloid Heroes'.

The mainly green cover – designed by Davis, Wade & Farrell – showed a heavily retouched photo of Ray with cartoon images of film stars at the top and audience members at the bottom. The reverse had the album subtitle – *Everybody's A Star* – the tracklist and retouched images of the five Kinks.

The album shows a slight change in Ray's writing style, as he becomes more theatrical and, in some places, quite camp. Thematically, it explores the realities of rockstar life, the monotony of touring, bad food and the inequality of the classes. Ray has admitted since that while recording this album, he had his mind on the next one: which would continue his string of concept albums but with added theatrics.

'Here Comes Yet Another Day' (Davies)
The album starts with this rocking song, with the horn section adding some power. It's the most fitting start to this album which deals with life on the road and success – almost like a diary of life on the road. As the lyrics say, even when a new day comes, it's 'just like any other day'.

'Maximum Consumption' (Davies)
A bluesy song about the food excesses of living life on the road: you have to keep going and keep your energy levels up, you end up eating more food for fuel. This has a punchy beat with brass in the background and a rather quirlky slide guitar.

'Unreal Reality' (Davies)
This is lyrically similar to 'Here Comes Yet Another Day'. This brass-heavy song has a funereal start but picks up the tempo. The singer is looking around him and asking whether this is all real or an illusion?

'Hot Potatoes' (Davies)
The B-side to the single 'Celluloid Heroes'.
After a tour – where you're in a bubble and eating hotel food – you have to go back home and get used to ordinary food and day-to-day life again. The singer is home after a tour but has to get a job. 'Hot Potatoes' is another song with the kind of bluesy feel that Ray was fond of writing.

Above: The Kinks in 1965. Ray (centre top) with (L-R.) Mick Avory, Dave Davies, Pete Quaife.*(Alamy)*

Left: *Kinks*. The first album with a typical Kinks pose of the time. It was obviously not a big-budget shoot. (*Pye Records / Castle Communications*)

Right: They could have smiled at least for *Kinda Kinks* while Dave checks out Pete's shoes. (*Pye Records / Castle Communications*)

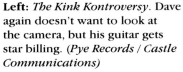

Left: *The Kink Kontroversy*. Dave again doesn't want to look at the camera, but his guitar gets star billing. (*Pye Records / Castle Communications*)

Right: Psychedelia enters the fray, and *Face To Face* is very much of the era. There are no band pictures. (*Pye Records / Castle Communications*)

Left: *Something Else By The Kinks*. We're Back to images of the band, and Dave is finally looking at the camera! (*Pye Records / Castle Communications*)

Right: *Live At Kelvin Hall.* The montage of images from the show give no doubt that this is a live album. (*Pye Records / Castle Communications*)

Left: *Village Green Preservation Society*. Arguably The Kinks' best album, the cover gives no indication of the delights within. (*Pye Records / Castle Communications*)

Right: *Arthur* has some patriotic items on the cover and a sepia-tint to evoke the past. (*Pye Records / Castle Communications*)

Left: *Lola Versus Powerman*. The Da Vinci-inspired cover is striking, as is the anger in the album's lyrics. (*Pye Records / Castle Communications*)

Right: Percy was The Kinks' Pye swansong and features the very colourful poster from the film. It's probably the most 'forgotten' album in the band's canon. (*Pye Records / Castle Communications*)

Left: The relaxed vibe of the pub setting on the cover of *Muswell Hillbillies* illustrates one of the band's most personal albums. (*RCA / Konk / Velvel*)

Right: The garish and cartoonish cover to *Everybody's In Showbiz* pays tribute to some cinema greats. (*RCA / Konk / Velvel*)

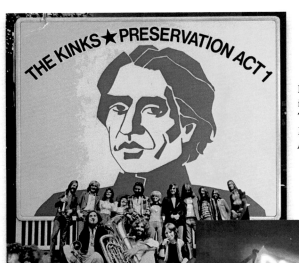

Left: *Preservation Act 1*. The first in a series of concept albums. The band shot is overlooked by Mr Flash on a billboard. (*RCA / Konk / Velvel*)

Right: We return to the billboard for *Preservation Act 2* as Ray looks over the desolation caused by the warring factions on the album. (*RCA / Konk / Velvel*)

Left: *Soap Opera*. The softer colours on the cover denote the fact that the concept of the album is more palatable than the previous two. (*RCA / Konk / Velvel*)

Right: In keeping with the 'school' theme of the *Schoolboys In Disgrace* album, we have a naughty schoolboy with the wicked headmaster in silhouette. (*RCA / Konk / Velvel*)

Left: *Sleepwalker* is the third album to feature only Ray on the front cover – leaving us with no doubt who the leader of The Kinks is. (*Arista / Konk / Velvel*)

Right: *Misfits* again features a solo Ray on the front (although Dave is on the back). It's a visually striking image for your author's favourite Kinks' album. (*Arista / Konk / Velvel*)

Left: Ray Davies performing 'Lola' on the BBC-TV show *Top of the Pops*. Broadcast on 18 June 1970, he is using his newly-acquired National Steel Resonator guitar.

Right: Dave Davies performing 'Lola' on *Top Of The Pops*, 18 June 1970.

Left: Mick Avory, concentrating on laying down the beat for 'Lola' on *Top Of The Pops*.

Right: The reliable John 'Nobby' Dalton playing the bass on 'Lola' on *Top Of The Pops*.

Left: Dave Davies concentrating on his finger-work on BBC-TV's *The Old Grey Whistle Test*, broadcast on 6 April 1977.

Right: Ray on *The Old Grey Whistle Test* in 1977.

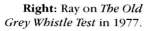

Left: The band was beginning to have greater success in America as *Low Budget* became their highest-placed album in the US charts. (*Arista / Konk / Velvel*)

Right: *One For The Road*. Ray on the front (and Dave on the back) as the band transitions from the 1970s to the 1980s. (*Arista / Konk / Velvel*)

Left: *Give The People What They Want* was the first of two 'graffiti' styled covers as Ray (solo again) runs away from the wall of Konk Studio. (*Arista / Konk / Velvel*)

Right: *State Of Confusion*. The whole band get a look in this time as Konk Studios gets defaced again. (*Arista / Konk / Velvel*)

Left: *Word Of Mouth*. Count the mouths: I make it nine. (*Arista / Konk / Velvel*)

Right: Ray addresses 80s Britain on *Think Visual* with a suitably stark cover. What the female bodybuilder is doing there is mystifying. (*MCA Records*)

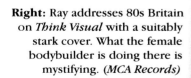

Left: *Live – The Road*. Again, the design is a little predictable. It's also a rather difficult album to track down these days. (*London Records*)

Right: *UK Jive*. With the band's impetus of the early eighties starting to slow, we get an 'English' album with Ray in a despondent mood. The Union Jack handkerchief and Cuban heel boots on the cover denote a different era. (*London Records*)

Left: Both Ray and Dave appear on *Phobia* – perhaps the most disturbing cover of any Kinks album. It's good, though. (*Sony / Columbia Records*)

Right: *To The Bone*. A pretty bland cover for the most recent Kinks' album to date. Hopefully, the hands are Ray and Dave together. (*Konk Records*)

Left: *Waterloo Sunset – The Songs Of Ray Davies* album cover. The companion CD to *The Singles Collection*. (*Castle Communications*)

Right: *The Kinks At The BBC* box set cover. The cover design is supposed to look like the *Radio Times* (the BBC's Television listings magazine). (*Sanctuary Records*)

Left: A letter from Ray Davies to Olga Ruocco, thinking her for liking the latest release, circa 1965. (*Olga Ruocco*)

Right: The author with Mick Avory and John Dalton at Preston Guildhall, 11 February 2016. (*Michaela Hutchinson*)

GREETINGS
from the Kinks
and everyone at
their office.

Left: A greetings card from The Kinks' office, signed by Ray Davies, Dave Davies, Mick Avory, John Gosling and Andy Pyle. (*Olga Ruocco*)

Right: The Kinks at the BBC – 1969. (L-R) John Dalton, Mick Avory, Dave Davies, Ray Davies. (*Kinks Fan Club Facebook Page*)

Below: A badge collection to promote the 50th-anniversary release of the *Village Green* album. (*Martin Hutchinson*)

THE KINKS ARE THE VILLAGE GREEN PRESERVATION SOCIETY

50TH ANNIVERSARY REMASTERED EDITIONS
AVAILABLE:
OCTOBER 26, 2018

BMG

Right: Ray Davies being knighted by HRH The Prince of Wales in March 2017. (*Kinks Fan Club Facebook Page*)

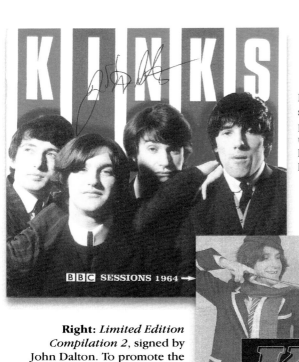

Left: *BBC Sessions 1964 – 1977*, signed by John Dalton. In promoting The Kinks, designers usually go for a 'British' feel, hence the red, white and blue here. (*Sanctuary Records*)

Right: *Limited Edition Compilation 2*, signed by John Dalton. To promote the reissue campaign for the RCA and Arista albums, a couple of promotional CDs were sent out. (*Konk / Velvel*)

Left: *The Singles Collection*, signed by John Dalton. A generic band photo and the companion to the *Songs Of Ray Davies* album. (*Castle Communications*)

'Sitting In My Hotel' (Davies)
B-side to 'Sweet Lady Genevieve'.

This is one of Ray's more introspective songs, dealing with the cost of fame – the loneliness and isolation caused by being away so long and how you can lose some of your identity. 'If my friends could see me now'. It is mainly a piano ballad. The song was almost offered to some MOR singers, notably the crooner Andy Williams, but Ray would've had to amend the lyric to remove the slang ('strides' and 'daisy roots'), and he refused.

'Motorway' (Davies)
This idea came to Ray whilst driving home from an appearance at Wigan's Bickershaw Festival on 6 May 1972. It's about the disadvantages of driving on the motorway when travelling between gigs – the bad food, weak coffee and petrol fumes are all mentioned. This song – which has a jaunty country sound – is a bit of comic relief on what is in fact, quite a dark album.

'You Don't Know My Name' (Dave Davies)
The B-side to 'Supersonic Rocket Ship'.

Dave is singing about how he was feeling at the time. He wasn't enjoying touring, as it kept him away from his family. But when he asks 'Does anybody know my name?', is it a veiled barb directed at the way Ray has in effect become The Kinks, and the rest of the band, including Dave, is just his backing band? It is an impassioned plea in the form of an uptempo blues song.

'Supersonic Rocket Ship' (Davies)
UK release: RCA Victor Records, RCA 2211, 5 May 1972 (UK), 1 September 1972 (US). Producer: Ray Davies. Chart positions: UK: 16, US: 111, Australia: 16

There's a great party-like calypso feel on this track, with steel drums and Ray's Resonator guitar providing the distinctive sound. It was the first song recorded for the album at a session in February, but some of the recording was accidentally wiped, so they had to redo it. The single reached 16 in the UK charts and would be the band's last sizeable hit for over a decade. And though it reached the top 10 in Boston, it only reached 111 in the States.

The ship will take the singer to a simpler place where there is no class. The inference is that the ship is in fact, the Concorde (as there was only one class on Concorde). This was Ray kicking the class system again. The irony being that he had to fly on the Concorde himself when delivering the tapes to RCA in New York.

'Look A Little On The Sunny Side' (Davies)
The singer realises that you can't please everyone all the time. 'You gotta be shrewd, you gotta be strong' and 'convince yourself you're not wrong and come out the other side. Brass is to the fore in this vaudevillian romp.

'Celluloid Heroes' (Davies)

UK release: RCA Victor Records, RCA 2299, 24 November 1972. Producer: Ray
Davies. Chart positions: Did not chart

This has become one of The Kinks' most important songs and always appeared
in the live set. The band had recorded the backing track and vocal the night
before jetting to New York to deliver the album master tapes. The UK single has
the full 6:19 version, while the US mix was about two minutes shorter. Despite
its standing in the Kinks canon, the single failed to chart on either side of the
Atlantic. It's a slow ballad about the transitory nature of fame. The song name-
checks many Hollywood stars and their inclusion on the Hollywood Walk of
Fame on Hollywood Boulevard.

Original Live Tracks

'Top Of The Pops' (Live) (Davies), 'Brainwashed' (Live) (Davies), 'Mr. Wonderful'
(Live) (Bock, Weiss, Holofcener), 'Acute Schizophrenia Paranoia Blues' (Live)
(Davies), 'Holiday' (Live) (Davies), 'Muswell Hillbilly' (Live) (Davies), 'Alcohol'
(Live) (Davies), 'Banana Boat Song (Trad.)' (Live) (Burgie, Attaway), 'Skin And
Bone' (Live) (Davies), 'Baby Face' (Live) (Davis, Akst), 'Lola' (Live) (Davies)

Bonus Tracks from the 1998 reissue on Konk/Velvel (63467-79720-2)

'Till The End Of The Day' (Live) (Davies), 'She's Bought A Hat Like Princess
Marina' (Live) (Davies)

Recorded on 2 and 3 March 1972 at Carnegie Hall, this showed a sample of
the newer songs that were in the live set at the time. Amongst the Ray Davies
songs are snippets of three songs from a previous era – 'Mr. Wonderful' (A hit
for Peggy Lee in 1956, originally sung by Sammy Davis Jr. in the 1956 Broadway
musical of the same name); 'Baby Face' (Written in 1926 and recorded by
many artists, most notably Al Jolson) and 'Banana Boat Song' (A Jamaican folk
song made popular by Harry Belafonte in 1956, with a comedy version by
Stan Freberg in 1957). Ray would use the refrain 'Day-O' as part of audience
participation in Kinks shows for years to come. What's also notable about these
live recordings is that Ray's becoming more outgoing and showy: a trait that
would be developed over the next few years.

In 2016, RCA/Legacy reissued the album as a double CD. The first disc had the
original album. The two Velvel bonus tracks were included on the second disc
along with 11 live tracks from the two Carnegie Hall concerts. The track list for
the second Legacy CD is as follows (All songs written by Ray except where noted):

'Till The End Of The Day' (Live), 'You're Looking Fine' (Live), 'Get Back In Line'
(Live), 'Have A Cuppa Tea' (Live), 'Sunny Afternoon' (Live), 'Muswell Hillbilly'
(Live), 'Brainwashed' (Live), 'Acute Schizophrenia Paranoia Blues' (Live), 'Holiday'
(Live), 'Alcohol' (Live), 'Complicated Life' (Live), 'She's Bought A Hat Like Princess

Marina' (Live), 'Long Tall Shorty' (Live) (Herb Abramson, Don Covay) (Sung by Dave Davies), 'History' (An unreleased studio outtake recorded on 1 March 1973), 'Supersonic Rocket Ship' (Alternate mix), 'Unreal Reality' (Alternate mix), 'Sophisticated Lady' (An early version of 'Money Talks' which would later appear on the album ***Preservation Act 2***)

Preservation Act 1 (1973)

Personnel:
Ray Davies: vocals, guitar, harmonica
Dave Davies: lead guitar, vocals
John Dalton: bass
Mick Avory: drums
John Gosling: keyboards
Additional personnel:
Alan Holmes: baritone saxophone, clarinet
Laurie Brown: trumpet, flute, tenor saxophone
John Beecham: trombone, tuba
Krysia Kocjan: backing vocals
Lee Pavey, Lewis Rich, Pamela Travis, Sue Brown: backing vocals
Producer: Raymond Douglas Davies
Running time: 39:16
Recorded at Konk Studios, London (May-July 1973)
Release date: 16 November 1973
Original UK label and catalogue number: RCA Victor Records SF8392
Chart positions: UK: –, US: 177, Australia: 92

The next two albums could almost be classed as one, as they are the two parts to one story. After five years, Ray returned to the village green concept to take it a stage further. However, it very nearly didn't happen, as the first part of 1973 wasn't the best time of his life.

January saw the performance of a full stage show based on the 1968 album *The Kinks Are The Village Green Preservation Society* at London's Theatre Royal in Drury Lane – with extra musicians and singers, extra songs and a full light show. Ray originally intended to tour the show, but it immediately went over budget, and in the end, following the Theatre Royal performance, he condensed the performance down to a 90-minute version which included a hits package.

Another project came to fruition in May when their Konk studios opened for business. The band toured, as usual, doing more TV shows and another sell-out concert at London's Royal Festival Hall in June. The low point came in late June when Ray's wife Rasa – along with their two daughters – left him. On 15 July, the band were due to perform a show at the White City Stadium in London. It was an awful day with unceasing rain. Ray – who still had no idea where Rasa and the girls were – was in a bad way. He hadn't eaten or slept for days, but somehow he got through the set. However, during the set he dropped the bombshell that he was retiring. In his own words, he was 'sick up to here with it all'. Nobody in the band knew about this beforehand, and he left the venue immediately afterwards. What is less well-known is that Ray then took an overdose and went to hospital. As he was in full stage garb when he arrived, the staff at the hospital didn't take him seriously: until he collapsed. They pumped his stomach and he was later discharged into the care of his brother Dave.

Any previous ill-feeling between the brothers was put aside as Dave nursed Ray back to health. They played music together and went on a short holiday to Denmark. Meanwhile, the rest of the band had no idea what was going to happen. But in September, Ray issued a statement that he was not retiring and that some live dates had been booked.

The band then returned to their new base Konk Studios and recommenced work on the new album. Ray's vision for the *Preservation* concept grew into a master plan for a triple album set, which eventually became the single album *Preservation Act 1*, followed by *Preservation Act 2,* which would be a double album. A lot of the tracks had already been recorded at Morgan Studios earlier in the year, but after returning from a US tour in May, Ray began mixing the album but was disappointed with what he heard. So in true Ray Davies fashion, he scrapped the tapes and started over, this time at Konk.

Two tracks from the early sessions had been cleared for release as a single in America in time for the tour. 'One Of The Survivors' was released there but only scraped to 108 (The Kinks would not have another singles chart entry in the US until 1976). It was backed with 'Scrapheap City': a song that would appear on *Preservation Act 2*.

Deciding that the whole premise for *Preservation* would be too big for one album release, Ray wanted the albums released eight months apart. In the end, the releases were six months apart in the US, and eight months apart in the UK. *Act 1* charted in America and Australia (just), and *Act 2* performed slightly better in the US. Neither album charted in Britain.

To the story. We are back with the village green, and there are various forces trying to buy and develop it. Mr. Flash is the face of capitalism. He wants to demolish the village green and build on it, thereby taking the villages' soul away. He is opposed by Mr. Black, who is the face of the socialists. The everyman character in the story, watching everything from the sidelines, is The Tramp, who is really Ray Davies himself. This first album charts the rise of Mr. Flash and his cronies, and we are left in a kind of limbo at the end of the album, as the story isn't finished, and we have to wait until *Preservation Act 2* to find out what happens.

The front cover is dominated by a yellow billboard with an image of Mr. Flash in red, looking astoundingly like Ray (who did, in fact, play the character in the stage version). In front of the billboard are the fourteen musicians who played on the album (taken with a fish-eye lens). The back cover is another fish-eye photo of the musicians, with a track list. Looking closely, I'm pretty sure that the shirt that Ray is wearing in the cover images is the one he wore at the White City show.

'Morning Song' (Davies)
A song similar in style to the beginning of Dvorak's New World Symphony. Ray hums while a female chorus backs him. You can almost see the sun rise over the village as The Tramp (Ray) makes his way around it.

'Daylight' (Davies)

A scene-setter. The village comes to life in the morning (It's funny, I can picture *Camberwick Green* in my head as I read the lyrics). It's a new day in the village and everything is much the same as always. Acoustic guitar plays as Ray duets with himself.

'Sweet Lady Genevieve' (Davies)

UK release: RCA Victor Records, RCA 2418, 21 September 1973. Producer: Ray Davies. Chart positions: Did not chart

A single only issued in the UK, but with no success. This mid-tempo rock song is sung by The Tramp. He left his lady (Genevieve) to travel as a vagabond. But now he's returned and hopes to reclaim his love – repentant about the way he treated her in the past.

'There's A Change In The Weather' (Davies)

This is sung by three different characters –Working Class Man, Middle Class Man and Upper Class Man. They have different outlooks, but they can all see that changes are coming to the village and storm clouds are gathering (as emphasised by the brass section).

'Where Are They Now?' (Davies)

The Tramp is back, and this is a lament for the people he knew about in days gone by who have now disappeared. The list includes teddy boys and Christine Keeler.

'One Of The Survivors' (Davies)

B-side to 'Sitting In The Midday Sun'.

One of the people who has survived is Johnny Thunder (from *The Village Green Preservation Society*). This rock and roll number tells us that he's still the same (but is older and has put on weight) and has no interest in moving on from the 1950s. It is sung (like nearly all the album) by Ray, but Dave joins in towards the climax of this out-and-out rock and roll pastiche. In America, 'Sweet Lady Genevieve' was the B-side.

'Cricket' (Davies)

Released as a B-side to 'Mirror Of Love' in 1974 in France.

All villages have their vicar, who is usually the pillar of the community. Here, the vicar is likening life to a game of cricket, with Satan as the demon bowler and to play him with a 'straight bat' (a cricketing analogy, usually meaning to do something in a straightforward and honest way). The vicar is accompanied by the brass section giving us some old-fashioned traditional jazz.

'Money And Corruption/I Am Your Man' (Davies)

The chorus (depicting the people of the village) have become fed up with being promised riches whilst the corrupt businessmen and politicians get all the money. Then Mr. Black stands up to be the people's saviour – stating his socialist ideals of working with the unions and working-man by nationalising companies. Everyone will have their creature comforts after his 'five-year plan'.

'Here Comes Flash' (Davies)
In a typical up-tempo (but in a way menacing) number, The Chorus of Scared Housewives tell us that Mr. Flash is coming. He appears to be an aggressive businessman who will smile at you then screw you over. He is out to get everything he can, and he is the face of capitalism.

'Sitting In The Midday Sun' (Davies)
UK release: RCA Victor Records, RCA 2387, August 1973. Producer: Ray Davies. Chart positions: Did not chart
This a relaxing song and has been described as a sequel to 'Sitting By The Riverside' from the *Village Green* album. The Tramp is content to sit in the midday sun. He is just sitting and watching everything go by and has no worries.

'Demolition' (Davies)
Here we meet Mr. Flash and his cronies, who are setting out their campaign to buy everything up cheaply, using compulsory purchase orders and demolishing the old to make way for the new. This is where the first act finishes. Mr. Flash has apparently won. He's bought up the town, and nobody seems to be able to stand in his way. Can the village green be saved? We must wait for the second act. Luckily, we didn't have too long to wait. At the start of this track, Mr Flash and his Cronies are all played by Ray with different characters outlining their aims before the girl chorus and Dave enter the fray.

Bonus Tracks from the 1998 reissue on Konk/Velvel (63467-79721-2)
'Preservation' (Single edit) (Davies)
This 1970s-style rocker actually tells the whole story of *Preservation*. It was recorded at Konk in October 1974 and released as a single in America with 'Salvation Road' (a song from *Preservation Act 2*) on the B-side.

'One Of The Survivors' (Single edit) (Davies)
This is the original recording of the track which was scrapped from the album. It was released as a single in the US, b/w 'Scrapheap City' (which would appear on *Preservation Act 2*).

Preservation Act 2 (1974)

Personnel:
Ray Davies: vocals, guitar
Dave Davies: lead guitar, vocals
John Dalton: bass
Mick Avory: drums
John Gosling: keyboards
Additional personnel:
Alan Holmes: baritone saxophone, clarinet
Laurie Brown: trumpet, flute, tenor saxophone
John Beecham: trombone, tuba
Maryann Price: backing vocals
Angi Girton: backing vocals
Pamela Travis: backing vocals
Sue Brown: backing vocals
Christopher Timothy: announcer
Chris Musk: reporter
Producer: Raymond Douglas Davies
Running time: 67:00
Recorded at Konk Studios, London (January-March 1974)
Release dates: UK: 26 July 1974, US: 8 May 1974
Original UK label and catalogue number: RCA Victor Records LPL2 5040
Chart positions: UK: –, US: 114

The first part of 1974 saw The Kinks holed up in Konk Studios recording
Preservation Act 2, and by the time the album was finished in March, Dave
thought Ray had gotten his theatrical and conceptual urges out of his system,
but he hadn't. In April, the band toured America with the *Preservation* show.
Some of the shows were a bit shambolic, as alcohol consumption was rather
high, and Ray was a little erratic, sometimes stopping the band mid-song.
Some shows were cancelled due to him having back problems. The band
as a whole were beginning to tire of Ray's theatrical demands, as they were
required to play parts in the show, something they were less than comfortable
with.

On 25 July, the band were in Granada TV Studios in Manchester, filming a
TV special called *Starmaker*, and as this formed the basis of The Kinks' next
album, I'll deal with it in the appropriate place. The months following the
release of *Preservation Act 2* were busy, as the band was signing acts for their
own record label, also called Konk. Much of 1974 was spent recording and
producing other acts.

Ray was in the middle of a very prolific period. As soon as the second
Preservation album been released, the band were in Konk Studios recording
the next album (More about which later). Ray also remarried. He and Rasa
divorced at the end of 1973, and he married his second wife, Yvonne Gunner,

in November 1974. This marriage was kept secret from the public right up until their divorce in 1981.

Sadly, *Preservation Act 2* wasn't a hit, and made a poor showing even in America, although it did slightly better than *Act 1* in the charts. It carries on the story from the previous album with the battle between capitalism (Mr. Flash) and socialism (Mr. Black). More characters are introduced, and the whole album has a narrative with spoken announcements throughout. Of course, The Tramp is keeping his eye on events as they unfold. The story concludes with Mr. Black ousting Mr. Flash. But things may not have turned out for the better, as it seems that Mr. Black's socialism has mutated into communism and a dictatorship.

The front cover has a massive billboard with the title and band name, with Ray as Mr. Flash overlooking a wasteland. The reverse has the band and three 'floosies' against the wasteland. The band are all in costume – Ray as Mr. Flash, Dave Davies and Mick Avory were two spivs (a 'spiv' is a slang word for a petty criminal, usually flashily dressed, who deals In illicit goods. Although coined in a crime novel of 1934, the term became popular in the Second World War describing someone who dealt in the 'black market'). John Gosling was the vicar and John Dalton was a revolutionary. The photographer was Chris Hopper, art direction was by Pat Doyle, and the designer was Bob Searles.

'Announcement' (Davies)
A fanfare heralds a news announcement (one of several by Christopher Timothy) telling us that there are rumours of a 'People's Army' led by Commander Black, who is planning to overthrow the government, headed by Mr. Flash.

'Introduction To Solution' (Davies)
A funky song in which The Tramp tells us what he's seeing, and it's all going wrong – the corruptness of Mr. Flash whilst the people grow hungry. He states that a 'military coup has been long overdue'.

'When A Solution Comes' (Davies)
A slower number which introduces us to Mr. Black. He's in an attic somewhere in suburbia, biding his time as he makes his plans for the solution to Mr. Flash.

'Money Talks' (Davies)
Mr. Flash and the Spivs and Floosies are in his den, which is a converted office in the back of a nightclub. Mr. Flash is commenting on how money can buy everything. Money talks and everybody listens.

This slow rocker has Dave singing in a high register alongside Ray. It was also released as a single in America, b/w 'Here Comes Flash' from the previous album.

'Announcement' (Davies)
There's no fanfare as the announcer states that Mr. Black is about to make a public statement. There are crowd sound effects as Mr. Black takes the stage and commentary by Chris Musk.

'Shepherds Of The Nation' (Davies)
B-side to 'Holiday Romance' in 1974.
This is sung by Mr. Black and The Do-Gooders in an almost preaching voice. Mr. Black states that he and his followers are against sin and corruption, that they will 'cast out Satan' and
"let righteousness prevail".

'Scum Of The Earth' (Davies)
Mr. Flash comments that even though he has made money and been successful, he's only human, and doesn't deserve to be called 'scum of the earth', and deep down, we are all the same. The Spivs and Floosies agree with him. It's sung partially in a melodramatic voice; speeding up when he lists his human qualities.

'Second-Hand Car Spiv' (Davies)
The Spiv in question tells us how he left school with nothing and worked his way up, starting with secondhand cars and going into property and stocks and shares. He then states that he's in charge of the country as a whole, which of course, means that the Spiv is actually Mr. Flash. Musically, it's a vaudevillian sing-song with brass thrown in at intervals to give a bit of light and shade. A bit of the fanfare from the first announcement pops up at the end.

'He's Evil' (Davies)
B-side to 'Mirror Of Love'.
With a chorus of His Followers, Mr. Black gives a party political broadcast, warning the population about what Mr. Flash is really like. 'He's Evil' is a slice of 1970s rock/funk with the electric piano that was almost ever-present in singles at the time.

'Mirror Of Love' (Davies)
UK release: RCA Victor Records, RCA 5015, 26 July 1974. Producer: Ray Davies. Chart positions: Did not chart
This is a jazzy little number, with honky-tonk piano and brass to the fore, sung by Ray as Belle (Mr. Flash's special woman). It's strange is that Marianne Price didn't sing this, as she sings as Belle on 'Nothing Lasts Forever' and 'Scrapheap City'. Belle likes what she sees in the mirror, and wonders why Mr. Flash treats her so badly.

'Announcement' (Davies)
The announcement of Mr. Black winning a battle indicates that the fight
between him and Mr. Flash has become violent, and the country is perhaps in
the throes of a civil war.

'Nobody Gives' (Davies)
In this mid-tempo rocker, The Tramp wonders why nobody compromises
('gives') anymore. He likens the situation to the general strike in 1925 and the
Second World War, where nobody listened to each other.

'Oh Where Oh Where Is Love?' (Davies)
The Tramp joins the Do-Gooders in this lament about the loss of love, hope,
respect and faith. It seems that in The Tramp, Ray is trying to be the voice of
reason.

'Flash's Dream (The Final Elbow)' (Davies)
Mr. Flash is beginning to lose ground in the battles, and Mr. Black's forces
are closing in. He falls into a drunken stupor and has an argument with his
soul, who visits him in a dream. Flash tries to justify himself with no success.
Vocal effects depict the voice of his soul. This is a spoken segment with some
snippets of chorus in the background and in the last third of the song, his
internal battle is accompanied by trumpets and the full band, with the chorus
introducing snippets of 'Revolution'.

'Flash's Confession' (Davies)
With an intro containing a snippet of 'Here Comes Flash', Mr. Flash confesses
all in this menacing song, with tympani and synthesizer. He has looked at
himself, and he has become the person that he once despised.

'Nothing Lasts Forever' (Davies)
Mr. Flash goes on the run and turns to Belle (Marianne Price) for help, but
Belle has changed. In this touching song – despite Mr. Flash looking back on
the good times they shared – Belle tells him that 'nothing lasts forever' and she
no longer feels anything for him. Mr. Flash takes his leave, telling her that his
love for her will never die.

'Announcement' (Davies)
The fanfare heralds the end of the conflict. Mr. Flash and his men will be tried
for treason.

'Artificial Man' (Davies)
Mr. Flash is to be taken to a secret hideout to have his brain cleansed. He wants
to stay the way he is and doesn't want to be an artificial man. However, Mr.

Black and a Mad Scientist tell him that this is the world they are attempting to build – an Orwellian vision where everyone is programmed and kept under scrutiny, leaving us to wonder whether Mr. Black is the saviour after all. Despite the lyrical content being so chilling, this is quite an up-tempo and happy-sounding song.

'Scrapheap City' (Davies)

Belle sings this mock-country song as Mr. Flash's empire is being dismantled. Despite the battle against him, everything has been demolished anyway, and there is 'no quality'. They are erecting 'concrete monstrosities' and killing off all the animals. So, in effect, Mr. Black's regime has done exactly what Mr. Flash did. So we are no better off.

'Announcement' (Davies)

A final announcement which puts the country under martial law, with curfews, rationing and a shutdown of all entertainment.

'Salvation Road' (Davies)

This deceptively-jaunty song is the new national anthem. 'The workers of the world shall give the profits to the people'. Has the country become a communist state?

   And so the story ends, and it seems that the people have not won after all.

Bonus Tracks from the 1998 reissue on Konk/Velvel (63467-79722-2)

'Mirror Of Love' (Alternative mix) (Davies)

The version that was released as a single, with additional horns and background singers.

'Slum Kids' (Take 1) (Live, March 1979) (Davies)

This was in the original stage version of *Preservation* but never made it to the album. This slow shuffle was also performed in The Kinks' Christmas concert in 1977.

The Kinks Present A Soap Opera (1975)

Personnel:
Ray Davies: vocals, guitar,
Dave Davies: lead guitar, vocals
John Dalton: bass
Mick Avory: drums
John Gosling: keyboards
Additional personnel:
June Ritchie: vocals
Alan Holmes: saxophone
Laurie Brown: trumpet
John Beecham: trombone
Shirlie Roden, Lyndsey Moore, Pamela Travis: backing vocals
Producer: Raymond Douglas Davies
Running time: 37:30
Recorded at Konk Studios, London (August-October 1974)
Release dates: UK: 16 May 1975, US: 25 April 1975
Original UK label and catalogue number: RCA Victor Records SF 8411
Chart positions: UK: –, US: 51

While recording and touring *Preservation*, Ray had also been working on songs for a Granada TV special. Directed by Peter Plummer (who had won a BAFTA award for *Harlequin* in 1973) and choreographed by Dougie Squires, *Starmaker* appears to be about a pop star who decides to become an ordinary man and write about it for an album. In actual fact, it's the story of 36-year-old accountant Norman Grey, who fantasises that he is a pop star and *becomes* ordinary to make an album. In a way, it's Ray pretending to be someone who wants to be, well, *Ray*.

The show was filmed as part of Granada's *Late Night Drama* slot in front of an audience on 25 July 1974 (following two days of rehearsals) and broadcast on 4 September. Ray, of course, had the starring role, with June Ritchie playing his wife Andrea, who is ten years younger. They were the only proper acting roles in the production, which lasts just over half an hour. The rest of the cast is made up of dancers, backing singers and The Kinks. Unfortunately, this was another bone of contention within the rest of the band, as they were hardly seen during the show and were more and more of the opinion that they were becoming little more than Ray's backing band. Even Dave – who was initially in favour of the theatrical shows – was becoming less than enamoured with his role.

Reviews for the TV show were lukewarm and having watched it, the show does look a bit rough and ready. Perhaps a full-fledged play (with or without music) would've been better, as the overall storyline is a good one. Most of the songs performed in the TV show appeared on the subsequent album. The ones omitted were: 'Underneath The Neon Sign', 'Holiday Romance' and 'Ducks On

The Wall'. Some others were either curtailed or combined in a medley: such as 'When Work Is Over' and 'Have Another Drink'.

After the TV show was in the can, the band carried on touring the *Preservation* albums. The first half of the show was a hits package, with both *Preservation* albums being condensed into a roughly-90-minute second half. Then when the band toured *A Soap Opera* in 1975, the show's first half included a couple of songs from the 'Preservation' albums – 'Here Comes Flash' and 'Mirror Of Love' – and the second half was the presentation of the new album.

Despite some reviewers stating the new album's songs were a bit lacklustre, Pete Townshend of The Who thought it was 'unbelievable' (in a good way). Also, it sold better, and some people probably thought the story fit the songs better (or vice versa), and it wasn't as unwieldy as the *Preservation* concept. In any event, it did better in the American charts, scaling to the dizzy heights of 51: the band's best chart placing since *Percy* four years previous. As the band concentrated its efforts in America, the album failed to make an impression in England, and they only played ten UK shows to showcase it before taking a much-needed five-month break from touring.

The Kinks Present A Soap Opera started a short-lived trend of album titles starting with *The Kinks Present*, as the albums were best suited to being presented as live shows rather than just a set of recorded songs. Happily, this trend would only apply to two albums before – like the theatrical concepts themselves – being retired. But in my opinion, the songs – like those of the next album – are brilliant examples of Ray Davies at his very best and most insightful. To me, they are not merely a musical – they illustrate a story and, as such, have the ability to stand apart from the live shows. The album does have snippets of dialogue both in and between the songs, all undertaken by Ray (as either The Starmaker or Norman) and June Ritchie.

Pat Doyle again directed the cover art, with illustrations by Joe Petagno. The front cover has the title above, and 'featuring Norman and the Starmaker' below a circular inset of the Starmaker's hand touching Norman's hand – a style copied from Michaelangelo's The Creation Of Adam which is on the ceiling of the Vatican's Sistine Chapel. Below the hands, are Norman and Andrea's mural of the ducks on the wall. The background of the cover, and that of the reverse (which has the track listing), is the sky. Inside the gatefold were the lyrics with more illustrations of the songs.

Three singles were taken from the album in the UK, but none charted.

'Everybody's A Star (Starmaker)' (Davies)

In the intro to the album, The Starmaker introduces himself and tells us that he will swap places with an ordinary man: Norman. The Starmaker will live an ordinary life and Norman will be a star. Ray's singing is commanding and full of theatrical intonation as though he's delivering the Sermon on the Mount. It's heavy with brass, organ and pomposity, and is just about the nearest The Kinks ever got to glam rock. However, where we would normally have Dave singing the high harmonies, we get the female singers: another thing that would have gotten on Dave's nerves.

This track was released as a single in the US, with 'Ordinary People' on the B-side. It didn't chart.

'Ordinary People' (Davies)
The Starmaker and Norman change places, and The Starmaker starts getting to grips with the normal world – cocoa before bedtime, and pyjamas – and introduces himself to Norman's wife. He sings one of the albums pivotal lines: 'No sacrifice is too great for art'. It has a musical backing straight out of 1950s doo-wop, with saxophones and a repeating piano riff.

'Rush Hour Blues' (Davies)
B-side to 'Ducks On The Wall'.
This song has a faster tempo, as Norman will be late for work if he doesn't hurry. Ray gives us a good insight into commuting, though it's doubtful he ever commuted anywhere. As with the whole album, the sound is tight, as the number of musicians had been scaled down slightly. Mick Avory's hi-hat ticks off the seconds throughout. A striking bass riff from John Dalton leads us towards the end, which has more of a blues feel than the earlier pace.

'Nine To Five' (Davies)
This lilting song tells of the supposed boredom of a nine to five job, but how does Ray know anything about working nine to five? 'Answering phones and dictating letters' sums it all up, really. He manages to convey the ongoing drudgery. The pace picks up as we segue into...

'When Work Is Over' (Davies)
After the day's work, off to the pub. Ray and the chorus sing along to a funky background.

'Have Another Drink' (Davies)
B-side to 'You Can't Stop The Music'.
Ray is suggesting that we use alcohol to cope with the stresses of a job and life in general – both the repetition of it, and the fast pace of getting the work done. 'Have Another Drink' is in a country style, with some great riffs and refrains, and along with 'Holiday Romance', 'Ducks On The Wall' and 'Rush Hour Blues', it is one of my personal favourites from the album.

'Underneath The Neon Sign' (Davies)
The Starmaker is beginning to question his own reality. Is it real or an illusion? It's a gentle, reflective number with melodic guitar and horns. Songs in this style would crop up regularly on The Kinks' later 1970s albums.

'Holiday Romance' (Davies)

UK release: RCA Victor Records, RCA 2478, 11 October 1974. Producer: Ray Davies.
Chart positions: Did not chart

Norman/Starmaker appears to be alone in this song, as he takes a holiday
and has a short romance with Lavinia. Here we are transported sonically to a
different time – maybe the 1920s or 1930s - which is a personal highlight of the
album with its strings, muted brass and Ray's crooning singing style. A striking
piece of absurdity is where Ray adopts a falsetto for Lavinia's speaking voice
instead of delegating it to one of the female singers. It was released as a single
in the UK and Japan but failed to chart.

'You Make It All Worthwhile' (Davies)

On his return from the office, The Starmaker says he doesn't like Norman's
job, but Andrea makes it all worthwhile. However, in a twist on the romantic
and thoughtful start, an argument starts when he says he hates Shepherd's pie
(but Norman loves it). He then says that Norman's office got on his nerves.
The long-suffering Andrea then finally snaps and tells him he is really Norman.
Norman starts smashing things and says he especially hates the duck mural
on the wall. John Gosling's organ-playing stands out as played in a minor key,
which seems to jar against the unfolding melodrama.

'Ducks On The Wall' (Davies)

UK release: RCA Victor Records, RCA 2546, 18 April 1975. Producer: Ray Davies.
Chart positions: Did not chart

A great rocking number which again failed to trouble the chart compilers.
Sadly, we have never discovered who supplied the duck quacks which feature
throughout. It's a rocking number in which Norman finally breaks and rails
against his lifestyle. He particularly hates the ducks on the wall but can't get rid
of them, as his wife loves them.

'(A) Face In The Crowd' (Davies)

Norman realises that he cannot live in a fantasy world anymore and has to face
reality. It's a full production number with strings and keyboards filling out the
sound.

'You Can't Stop The Music' (Davies)

UK release: RCA Victor Records, RCA 2567, 23 May 1975. Producer: Ray Davies.
Chart positions: Did not chart

Released as an (unsuccessful) single in The UK, Australia and The Netherlands,
this was the one song not sung by Ray in the TV show – Dave sang it at the
end and over the closing credits. The title becomes a refrain at the end, with
some great soloing from Dave. Even as Norman becomes normal again, there is
always someone fantasising about being a star, as you can never stop the music.

Bonus Tracks from the 1998 reissue on Konk/Velvel (63467-79723-2)

'Everybody's A Star (Starmaker)' (Mono mix) (Davies)

The version that was released as a US single (RCA Victor JB10251) in May 1975.

'Ordinary People' (Live) (Davies), 'You Make It All Worthwhile' (Live) (Davies), 'Underneath The Neon Sign' (Live) (Davies)

Three live tracks recorded at the New Victoria Theatre, London (14 June 1975). These tracks show how these songs had much more life in a live setting. 'Ordinary People' has Dave on lead vocal and at the same time supplying some fantastic solo guitar: something he discussed at length with Ray (in reality, fought over). Some of the vocal interaction gives scope for some humour, which doesn't come across on the record.

The Kinks Present Schoolboys In Disgrace (1975)

Personnel:
Ray Davies: vocals, guitar, piano
Dave Davies: lead guitar, vocals
John Dalton: bass
Mick Avory: drums
John Gosling: keyboards
Additional personnel:
Alan Holmes: saxophones
Nick Newall: tenor saxophone
John Beecham: trombone
Shirlie Roden, Debbie Doss, Pamela Travis: backing vocals
Producer: Raymond Douglas Davies
Running time: 36:26
Recorded at Konk Studios, London (August-October 1975)
Release dates: UK: 23 January 1976, US: 17 November 1975
Original UK label and catalogue number: RCA Victor Records RS 1028
Chart positions: UK: –, US: 45

1975 was a lucky year for Kinks fans in the US because they were to get a second new release, whilst British fans would have to wait until January 1976. Following the American shows of the *Preservation* albums and *A Soap Opera*, Ray began writing for what would turn out to be the last theatrical album. *The Kinks Present Schoolboys In Disgrace* was, in fact, a prequel to the *Preservation* trilogy, as we are told the story of the school days of Mr. Flash. It's Ray looking back – a recurring theme in his songwriting as we have seen – as he reminisces about times when all our decisions were made for us. Perhaps another reason for him looking back to the past was that in July 1975, Fred – Ray and Dave's father – died suddenly.

This new album would return to being more thematic, as – though there is a sort of storyline running through – all the songs could stand alone, and a couple of them would be in the Kinks' live set for some years afterwards. Even though we still had the brass section and female backing vocalists, this was The Kinks sounding more like the rock band it actually was, and this was one of the reasons that Dave Davies was more involved. Some of the songs – in particular 'I'm In Disgrace' – are based on Dave's experiences at school (He was expelled after getting his girlfriend pregnant) – in fact, he described it as 'a rebirth for the band'.

In October, once the recording was complete, the band took the show on the road in America, just prior to the album's November release there, and again it was presented in a theatrical format with UK band Steve Harley and Cockney Rebel as support. As with recent US tours, the shows were well-received, but Ray's moods were a bit erratic, which led to some of the touring party labelling him as 'God'. This led to some tension in the entourage, and even the normally placid John Dalton had the occasional flare-up. However, Steve Harley remembers the tour with fondness. Steve told me, 'We had a great time. Ray and Dave were like family, and we all got on very well. Ray was always a complex man. Deep and interesting. I like him very much'.

The album did better again, reaching 45 in America, but it wasn't as well-received in the UK, where it failed to chart. This is a great shame, as it's a great collection of songs that really brings back memories of being at school in the 1950s and 1960s. However, it reached a creditable 18 in the Netherlands. In January 1976, two singles were released from the album: 'I'm In Disgrace' in the US and 'No More Looking Back' in Britain. Neither charted.

Though the band was gaining more and more popularity in America, their profile in Britain was poor. This was in part due to Pye's ceaseless repackaging of their back catalogue. Everything The Kinks did was measured against the hits of the previous decade, and the band had moved on. A change of direction was needed.

The album cover art was again directed by Pat Doyle. The front cover has the words 'The Kinks Present' in the top-left corner, with 'Schoolboys In Disgrace' in yellow (in the style of broken wooden school rulers). A spotlight picks out a crying schoolboy who has just been given the cane (Remember the good old days of corporal punishment?) by the headmaster, who is in silhouette at the back. The illustration was by Colin 'Mickey' Finn, who would later create the two removal men in the Dire Straits video for 'Money For Nothing'. The back cover had the story of the album, a track listing and a photograph of the five main band members in school uniform (which they also wore when presenting the album on stage). The photo – taken by Chris Hopper – shows the band in green uniforms with the usual schoolboy accoutrements of caps, satchels and catapults.

Schoolboys In Disgrace was The Kinks' last studio album on RCA Records, although they would issue the compilation *Celluloid Heroes* in 1976. And strangely, when Konk/Velvel reissued all the RCA and Arista albums in 1998, this was one of only two albums that had no bonus tracks: the other being *Give The People What They Want*.

'Schooldays' (Davies)
A quiet and thoughtful song, with a background of organ from John Gosling, alongside the usual guitar, bass and drums. Ray asks us to remember what our own schooldays were like. The singer 'loathed the regulations and rules' but now concedes that they were 'the happiest days of your life'.

'Jack The Idiot Dunce' (Davies)
Released on the B-side of 'No More Looking Back' in the UK.
Debi Doss portrayed Jack in the live shows. As well as the humour of an awkward pupil, the song is an attack on bullying. Jack is awkward and clumsy but creates his own dance. He's also so stupid that he doesn't understand he's being bullied. But his mother is 'so proud of him'.

'Education' (Davies)

Going right back to the cavemen, we have to learn and be educated in order to do the things we want to do. At over seven minutes long and very wordy, this production piece tells us the value of education. It's not all plain sailing, as – in the words of the song – 'education drives me insane'. But the moral is, 'Everybody needs an education'. The closing refrain of 'Education' returns in the track 'Finale'.

'The First Time We Fall In Love' (Davies)

Another 1950s-style doo-wop song, as the singer reminisces about their first love affair. This song and 'Education' struck a chord (no pun intended) with me personally, as when I heard this album for the first time, I'd gone through the *first love* stage and also had recently left school. The song's stronger second half tells very accurately of the feelings when you fall out of love. Ray must've been channelling his feelings from when he and Rasa broke up.

'I'm In Disgrace' (Davies)

This is based on Dave being expelled and was particularly popular in America, where it was released as a single and performed in the live shows in years to come. The track sounds more like The Kinks from the 1960s, with Dave's crunching guitar prominent. Initially, he 'fell for your pretty face', but 'was it only infatuation?'.

'Headmaster' (Davies)

The schoolboy confesses to his bad behaviour and pleads for mercy. He starts off very humble and conciliatory before wailing, 'Don't make me take my trousers down'. It's a song that tells a story, like many on the album. There's some pretty funky guitar leading into the final verse.

'The Hard Way' (Davies)

B-side in the US and UK.

Ray donned a grotesque mask to play the part of the headmaster on stage – this caricature may have inspired Gerald Scarfe's depiction of the headmaster in Pink Floyd's *The Wall*. Ray based the song on his friends' visits to the employment office, where they were basically forced into jobs they weren't really suited to. According to The Headmaster, they are 'only fit to sweep the streets'. The song was a live favourite for years, as it had punk leanings and very much had the aggression of The Kinks from the previous decade. The powerful guitar mirrors the headmaster's anger.

'The Last Assembly' (Davies)

When we leave school, there is always that last time when all the pupils are all together. Ray was ill at his own last school assembly but struggled in as he felt it was important to be there for that one last time. John Gosling supplies the swirling organ against which the massed Kinks choir sing 'gather 'round/Come and join our last assembly'. It's similar in style to the hymn singing at all British school assemblies at that time.

'No More Looking Back' (Davies)

UK release: RCA Victor Records, RCM 1, 23 January 1976. Producer: Ray Davies. Chart positions: Did not chart

This was issued as a maxi-single with two tracks 'Jack, The Idiot Dunce' and 'The Hard Way' on the flip side. RCA were quite fond of these – reissuing David Bowie's 'Space Oddity' in 1975 as a maxi-single with 'Changes' and 'Velvet Goldmine' on the flip. The intro is played by a Rhodes electric piano, which The Kinks used very rarely, but is perfect for this song. And the brass and woodwind punctuating the chorus would be the last time The Mike Cotton Sound would appear on a Kinks album. This song addresses lost love. After leaving school, the boy sees things that remind him of his girlfriend, but she belongs to yesterday. The line 'yesterday's gone and that's a fact' is very poignant.

'Finale' (Davies)

The track title is fitting, as it was also a finale to this second stage of The Kinks' career. Basically, it's an elongated outro from the track 'Education'.

Sleepwalker (1977)

Personnel:
Ray Davies: lead and backing vocals, guitar, keyboards
Dave Davies: lead guitar, lead and backing vocals
John Dalton: bass
Mick Avory: drums, percussion
John Gosling: keyboards, backing vocals
Andy Pyle: bass ('Mr. Big Man')
Producer: Raymond Douglas Davies
Running time: 40:10
Recorded at Konk Studios, London (July-December 1976)
Release dates: UK: 25 February 1977, US: 12 February 1977
Original UK label and catalogue number: Arista Records SPARTY 1002
Chart positions: UK: –, US: 21

In Britain, The Kinks were still regarded as an act with an impressive back catalogue, but their more-recent material was being largely ignored. But in the States, their star was on the ascendency again, and Ray Davies wanted to capitalise on this. He felt that they (he in particular) had been cheated out of their just deserts by the ban that had rendered them unable to tour America from 1965 to 1969. With the success of the recent albums and theatrical tours, it was decided to concentrate their energies on making it big in the land of the free.

Album sales and chart placings had been steadily rising, and though Ray was happy that his visions were being well-received, a change was necessary. The music world was changing. In the UK – being a smaller country – music trends came and went. Glam rock was dominant in the first half of the decade but was being superseded by disco and punk. The Kinks could not be classed in these genres (although they had a couple of stabs at them, as we shall see later). In America – being such a massive country – the music remained (generally) more traditionally rock-based, and The Kinks fitted perfectly. They'd begun to produce music that was heavy with guitar riffs and more suited to what would become arena rock, where bands played in arenas holding upwards of 20,000 people.

To help the band make more of an impact, they signed with Clive Davis' Arista Records. Clive was the former vice-president of Columbia/CBS Music and founded Arista in 1974. He was known for making astute signings (With Columbia/CBS he'd signed Donovan, Tony Orlando and Dawn, Santana, Bruce Springsteen, Billy Joel and Aerosmith, among many others). Davis' skill at signing great artists continued at Arista with Barry Manilow, Aretha Franklin, Dionne Warwick, Eric Carmen, The Bay City Rollers and (later) Whitney Houston. So when The Kinks signed to the label in summer 1976, they were in great company.

Ray moved to New York and moved in next door to the Dakota building, thereby making him John Lennon's neighbour and within walking distance of

Clive Davis' office. The band started work immediately on their first album for their new label. Twenty songs were worked on during the sessions, though only nine were released on the original album. Four other tracks from the sessions were eventually released – two became B-sides to singles released in 1977 and 1978, and two were included on the Konk/Velvel 1998 reissue.

With the band having their own studio, they were able to record in a more-relaxed fashion, and that's probably why it took so long to record. But it also meant they had time to be more polished and did many takes and overdubs. They also pared the sound back to just the five members, with no brass section or backing singers – they were utilised only in live shows and then sparingly.

There was a downside to this, though – while the band were recording the album, it was done sporadically, and there was a hiatus in touring. This meant there was no money coming in for some of the band members. This proved too much for John Dalton, who had three children, and at one point, couldn't even pay his gas bill. In the end, he resigned from the band after recording all but one of the album's tracks.

Following auditions in December 1976 (Ray had to commute between New York (where he lived) and London (where he worked), Andy Pyle was recruited as the new bassist. Andy was born in Luton in 1945 and had been very active in bands and as a session musician. From 1969 to 1974, he was a member of the folk/blues-rock band Blodwyn Pig before joining the more bluesy Savoy Brown.

Released in February 1977, *Sleepwalker* was quite successful in the US, reaching a creditable 21 in the charts: The Kinks' highest US album chart placing so far. As usual, it didn't chart in the UK. Two singles were released from the album: 'Sleepwalker' and 'Juke Box Music'. The former scraped into the American top 50, but alas, that was it.

The front cover – which had art direction by John Dyer – was a monochrome image of a posing Ray (taken by James Wedge) with his face treated, so he seems to be wearing a clown mask. The band name and album title are top-left in a sloping script (by Hal Fiedler) that would be repeated on the next album. The overall design was by Bob Heimall.

Sleepwalker saw a return to more self-contained rock songs, thereby making it more commercial-sounding, although, thematically, Ray explores his moods and feelings.

'Life On The Road' (Davies)
The album has a slow start before launching into an up-tempo rock song. Ray returns to the theme of the rock and roll lifestyle and being on the road. It's also another London song, with a number of the capital's landmarks name-checked.

'Mr. Big Man' (Davies)
This is what could be classed as a power ballad. It's about a nameless 'big man' who has forgotten his roots and isn't the person he once was.

'Sleepwalker' (Davies)
UK release: Arista Records, ARISTA 97, 18 March 1977. Producer: Ray Davies. Chart positions: UK: –, US: 48, Australia: –

'Sleepwalker' was written by Ray about Ray (who was an insomniac) getting used to the 24-hour lifestyle of New York, where he was now living. It was originally about seven minutes long but was cut for the album. It's a definite rocker and fitting as the album's title track. The section at around 2.20 is interesting, with Ray's voice moving between left and right speaker. The band performed the song on the US TV show *Saturday Night Live* (with Steve Martin as host) along with a medley of hits on 26 February 1977.

'Brother' (Davies)
A big production number and a beautiful ballad. You'd think that with such a title it would be about Dave, but it's really Ray saying he's the brother of the man in the street. Fittingly, Ray and Dave's harmony vocals have never sounded better. Clive Davis of Arista Records wanted it to be released as a single because he believed it could be The Kinks' 'Bridge Over Troubled Water', but somehow it was never released as single. Your author's opinion is that maybe the marketing team at Arista thought that a ballad was not the way to go and that the band needed a more 'poppier' song to be released.

'Juke Box Music' (Davies)
UK release: Arista Records, ARISTA 114, 3 June 1977. Producer: Ray Davies, Chart positions: Did not chart

This was performed on the BBC TV music show *The Old Grey Whistle Test* along with 'Sleepwalker', 'Life Goes On', 'Stormy Sky', 'Full Moon' and 'Life On The Road' on 26 April 1977. (See *The Kinks At The BBC* - 2012.) Ray said this song is about a girl who listens to a jukebox all day and believes all the lyrics. She lets the music rule her life. But as the lyric points out, 'It's only juke box music'. Ray and Dave share lead vocals, and the song is about as rock-and-roll as Ray gets on the entire album.

'Sleepless Night' (Davies)
B-side to 'Juke Box Music'.

Sleepless Night' is another seven-minute track that was shortened. It was the B-side to 'Juke Box Music' in the UK and Germany. It's the only Dave Davies lead vocal on the *Sleepwalker* album and is full of his great guitar work. It's another insomniac song, but the cause of the protagonist's lack of sleep is that he's been jilted by a lover, and he can hear her with her new partner as they 'keep it up all night'.

'Stormy Sky' (Davies)
Ray is at his metaphorical best here. The title appears to be a threat, but as the music builds to a climax, there's a silver lining: after all, 'It's only a stormy sky'.

There is wonderful use of lead guitar doubling the melody line helps make this track one of the album's many highlights.

'Full Moon' (Davies)
B-side to 'Sleepwalker'.
In the atmospheric 'Full Moon', Ray uses the insomnia theme 'my midnight disguise' to explore how his mind wanders. Is he mad? It's perhaps a play on words with a 'full moon' by creating a form of lunacy.

'Life Goes On' (Davies)
B-side to 'Juke Box Music' in the US.
In a concert, Ray once described this as being about 'a man who tries to commit suicide, and fails'. Dave said the song is important to him, and he plays a very emotional solo. The track begins with a gentle organ and acoustic guitar intro. Deceptively, it's quite an upbeat song – life does go on, and the lyric tells us to 'Take that frown off your head/'Cause you're a long time dead'. There are some great harmonies, with Ray repeating himself rather like 'Row, Row, Row Your Boat'.

Bonus Tracks from the 1998 reissue on Konk/Velvel (63467-79725-2)

'Artificial Light' (Davies)
B-side to 'A Rock 'N' Roll Fantasy' from the next album.
'Artificial Light' is a disco number recorded at the *Sleepwalker* sessions, but it didn't see single release until it appeared as a B-side in the UK. It tells of how the singer notices a girl dancing under the lights. He says that you can let yourself go in the disco when you are shy outside. There is a nod to the psychedelic '60s in the instrumental section that has been phased.

'Prince Of The Punks' (Davies)
B-side of 'Father Christmas'.
'Prince Of The Punks' was recorded during sessions for the *Sleepwalker* album. It is really a dig at Konk artist Tom Robinson, who rose to fame in the punk rock era but, according to Ray, wasn't from that social strata: 'He's really middle-class, and he's just a phony'. The 'Prince' had also tried all the other genres of music ', from rock opera to Mantovani' before jumping on the punk bandwagon. Apparently, Tom was not pleased.

'The Poseur' (Davies)
This previously-unreleased track was originally meant to be the title track of the album. But in both sound and content, it would not have gelled with the rest of the album. The song is about a rather creepy person, maybe a cousin of the spiv character that Ray would later personify in the 'Come Dancing' video.

'On The Outside' (1977 Mix) (Davies)

One of Ray's isolationist songs, about a 'closet queen' who is afraid of coming out. The singer tries to persuade him to come out and be 'on the outside'. This theme would be partly returned to in 'Out Of The Wardrobe' on the next album. It's a mid-tempo song that Ray sings empathically.

'On The Outside' (1994 mix) (Davies)

This was released on the *Waterloo Sunset '94* EP.

Misfits (1978)

Personnel:
Ray Davies: vocals, guitar, piano, synthesizer
Dave Davies: lead guitar, vocals
Andy Pyle: bass
Mick Avory: drums, percussion
John Gosling: piano, organ, synthesizer
Additional personnel:
Nick Trevisik: drums ('Trust Your Heart', 'A Rock 'N' Roll Fantasy', 'Get Up')
John Dalton: bass ('In A Foreign Land')
Ron Lawrence: bass ('Live Life', 'A Rock 'N' Roll Fantasy', 'Get Up')
Zaine Griff: bass overdubs
Clem Cattini: drum overdubs
John Beecham: trombone ('Black Messiah')
Nick Newall: clarinet ('Black Messiah')
Mike Cotton: trumpet ('Black Messiah')
Producer: Raymond Douglas Davies
Running time: 40:29
Recorded at Konk Studios, London (August 1977-February 1978)
Release dates: UK: 19 May 1978, US: 17 May 1978
Original UK label and catalogue number: Arista Records SPARTY 1055
Chart positions: UK: –, US: 40, Australia: 79

Misfits was another transitional album for The Kinks because all was not well within the band. John Dalton had left (although he played bass on one track left over from the *Sleepwalker* sessions), and John Gosling wasn't happy. A number of reasons for his eventual departure were mooted. One was that – according to Dave Davies – Gosling's keyboards were limiting Dave's guitar-playing, something that John later said he was unaware of, and that if it was the case that Dave felt restricted by his playing, it wasn't intentional. The other – and more accurate – reason was that John thought The Kinks he knew and loved was no more because not only had his mate John Dalton left, but Mick Avory also appeared to be unhappy.

Gosling and Andy Pyle had also formed a band to fill in the time when they were not required to undertake Kinks duties. This band was called United and had been playing in London pubs during the spring of 1978. The final straw appeared to be when Ray Davies found out about the band: 'It was exhilarating', John said of the side-project shortly afterwards. 'But Ray somehow found out and started giving me a hard time during my last overdub session for *Misfits*'. The upshot was that both Andy and John departed from the ranks.

Mick Avory, on the other hand, had always felt an affinity with the 'hired help', and with Dalton, Gosling and then Pyle leaving, he became disenchanted and almost left himself. He had to be persuaded to take part in the tour to promote the finished album, but he didn't play on all the tracks. Nick Trevisick

– a session drummer and friend of Dave Davies – drummed on three tracks, and ex-Tornado member and renowned session man Clem Cattini played on 'Live Life' and completed the overdubs. Nick was from Devon (like Peter Quaife), and after his work on *Misfits*, he played on the 1980 Dave Davies solo album *AFL1-3603* (titled *PL 13603* in America, as the album was named after the catalogue number), and in 1982 hung up his drumsticks and moved full-time into writing and production. Clem was well-known to the band after playing on *The Kink Kontroversy* album and had also deputised on some live shows when Mick Avory was unwell.

When Andy Pyle left, Ron Lawrence from the Coventry folk scene was brought in to play bass on three tracks (and also played on Dave's 1980 solo album), and bass overdubs were by the New Zealand-born Zaine Griff. One track called for a horn section, and stalwarts John Beecham, Mike Newall and Mike Cotton, contributed to the track 'Black Messiah'.

The album was made up of shorter songs, but they all had a message pertaining to the title, and perhaps Ray was thinking of himself as a misfit, although one of the tracks was based on a friend. The subjects included depression ('Permanent Waves'), illness/allergies ('Hay Fever'), transvestism ('Out Of The Wardrobe'), racism ('A Rock 'N' Roll Messiah'), emigration ('In A Foreign Land') and exhortations to keep going ('Get Up', 'Live Life'). We also get a Dave Davies composition with 'Trust Your Heart' – his first writing contribution since 'You Don't Know My Name' from the 1972 *Everybody's In Showbiz* album.

The album cover is quite unusual and hard to describe. With photography by James Wedge, it's mainly blue with a beige section across the middle, giving the impression of the sky, desert and water. The front cover again features the band name and album title in the Hal Fiedler sloping script, with a photograph of Ray that has been treated to look like a fairground mirror. The reverse has a similarly-treated photo of Dave, but strangely, no track list. Inside the original release was a photo of the band, again treated, with everybody looking like physical misfits, along with the album lyrics.

Though moderately successful in the States, where it reached the top 40 (just), the album didn't chart in the UK. The singles fared little better, with only 'A Rock 'N' Roll Fantasy' charting in the US. Speaking of singles, the album was preceded by a non-album single in late-1977. 'Father Christmas' was Ray's take on the commercialisation of what was a religious festival, and gave the band a minor American hit reaching 41 in the charts.

The band toured the album from 26 May to 25 June 1978, and for that they needed some new touring musicians. On keyboards, they recruited Gordon Edwards, who'd played with The Pretty Things. Gordon was born in Southport, Merseyside, on Boxing Day 1947. He would only ever record one song with the band and was replaced in 1979 (more about which later). Sadly, he died in 2003. Jim Rodford was an experienced bassist and singer who'd once been in The Mike Cotton Sound and Argent with his cousin Rod Argent. (Rod had asked Jim to join The Zombies when the band was founded in 1962, and though Jim helped his cousin out with equipment, he declined to join.)

On a personal note, up to this point, all the music by The Kinks I had in my own collection was from the Pye reissues *The Golden Hour Of The Kinks* volumes one and two, the third volume with the unwieldy title *Lola, Percy And The Apeman Come Face To Face With The Village Green Preservation Society*, and one or two others from the 1970s. *Misfits* was the first album I bought when it was released, and I was hooked from the first note. Two years later, I managed (thanks to Pye reissuing all the original albums to take advantage of the mod renaissance) to acquire all the Kinks albums.

'Misfits' (Davies)
Single B-side to 'Black Messiah'
'Misfits' has a quiet and melodic opening and immediately addresses the overall theme of being a misfit. The song is in part about a friend of Ray's called Frank Smyth. Ray ran into Frank one night, walking the dog and invited him in, saying that 'He drank everything I had. I met him the next day and he looked remarkably fresh': hence the line 'You've been sleeping in a field, but you look well-rested'. The song also tells us there are lots of people who don't fit in, with Ray himself being an example: he was trying to fit into living in America at the time.

'Hay Fever' (Davies)
Recorded during the *Sleepwalker* sessions. With humour, Ray tells the story of a pollen-allergy sufferer in this up-tempo rocker. He laments that he can't go out because of the symptoms, as 'Hay fever is blocking up my head'. His accurate description of the allergy makes me wonder if Ray actually suffered from it himself.

'Black Messiah' (Davies)
UK release: Arista Records, ARIST 210, September 1978. Producer: Ray Davies.
Chart positions: Did not chart
What if God was black? This faux-reggae song puts this idea forward. There's even a disclaimer at the start saying, 'Everybody got the right to speak their mind/So don't shoot me for saying mine'.

'A Rock 'N' Roll Fantasy' (Davies)
UK release: Arista Records, ARIST 189, 19 May 1978. Producer: Ray Davies. Chart positions: UK: –, US: 30, Australia: –
The lead single from the *Misfits* album. Some people just like to retreat from life into music, and this is the story of such a person. 'Dan is a fan and he lives for our music', sings Ray, and he escapes from the world by turning 'his stereo way up high'. Gentle verses with more powerful choruses make it almost hymn-like. The line 'The King is dead' comes from Ray writing the song after

hearing about the death of Elvis Presley. According to Ray, it's also 'a very personal song about Dave and I'.

It became the band's best-selling US single since 'Lola' in 1970: reaching 30 there and in Canada. It was also released as the EP *The Kinks Misfit Record* in America, with 'Black Messiah', 'Misfits' and 'Permanent Waves'.

'In A Foreign Land' (Davies)
Single B-side to 'Live Life'
'In A Foreign Land' is another song recorded during the *Sleepwalker* sessions. This is the 1970s version of 'Sunny Afternoon', with the singer escaping the UK to avoid paying a massive amount of tax.

'Permanent Waves' (Davies)
In the mid-1970s, it became a trend for men to have their hair permed, and this mid-tempo pop song tells us of someone who is so depressed that his doctor advises him to improve his image and get his hair permed. Of course, Ray has to add a twist, and the perm gets washed out. But the protagonist has cheered up and will get his hair permed again.

I love the bass synth on this track. This song resonated with me personally, as on the day I bought the album, I had my own hair permed (It was purely coincidental, as I got the album a couple of hours after my appointment at the hairdresser).

'Live Life' (Davies)
UK release: Arista Records, ARIST 199, 14 July 1978. Producer: Ray Davies. Chart positions: Did not chart
There were a lot of bad things in the news around the mid-1970s, and Ray lists a few of them here. But he tells us not to lose our heads and to just 'be yourself' and live life on your own terms. This was also the B-side to 'A Rock 'N' Roll Fantasy' in the US. Dave has stated that 'Live Life' is one of his favourite tracks and that 'Clem Cattini did a great job playing drums on this'.

'Out Of The Wardrobe' (Davies)
Ray returns to a subject he addressed in 'Lola'. In this story of a transvestite called Dick coming out, the man in question has been married for over ten years to Betty Lou, who quite understandably is a little confused. But then she does the same, and their relationship is refreshed. There's some excellent guitar work from Dave on both electric and acoustic guitars on this reflective song, and it's a great story too.

'Trust Your Heart' (Dave Davies)
To be honest, this is not my favourite song on the album, and the stylus always jumped at the start. It's Dave's sole writing contribution to the album, and he

also supplies the lead vocal, which is rather shouty and harsh towards the end, after a deceptively-plaintive first three-quarters.

'Get Up' (Davies)
The album ends on an up with this inspirational rocker, exhorting the downtrodden 'little men' to get up and assert themselves. The intro sounds a little like The Who, with Dave using feedback and fuzz to get the correct guitar sound.

Bonus Tracks from the 1998 reissue on Konk/Velvel (63467-79726-2)
'Black Messiah' (Single remix) (Davies)
This is the version released as a single in the UK. It's shorter than the album version by 24 seconds.

'Father Christmas' (Davies)
UK release: Arista Records, ARISTA 153 25 November 1977 (UK), 8 December 1977 (US). Producer: Ray Davies. Chart positions: UK: −, US: 41, Australia: −
The Kinks had never done a Christmas single, and of course, Ray wouldn't have it all nicey-nicey, would he? No. In Ray's version, Santa is mugged, and the kids just want money as they and their families don't have any. 'Save all the toys for the little rich boys', they sing. The opening is nice and Christmassy, though, with piano and sleigh bells. At the height of punk, this should've been a massive hit, but it only got to 41 in the States. Ray performed it with great energy in The Kinks' Christmas Concert on BBC's *The Old Grey Whistle Test*.

'A Rock 'N' Roll Fantasy' (US single edit) (Davies)
A full minute and two seconds were edited from the album track for this version.

'Live Life' (US single mix) (Davies)
61 seconds were edited from the album track for this US single version.

'Jack, The Idiot Dunce' (Davies)
'Jack, The Idiot Dunce' is a nice slice of 1950s-style rock and roll, with dance moves included, it's also a fun and upbeat song, as opposed to the harshness and despair in 'The Hard Way'.

Low Budget (1979)

Personnel:
Ray Davies: vocals, guitar, keyboards
Dave Davies: lead guitar, backing vocals
Jim Rodford: bass, backing vocals
Mick Avory: drums
Additional personnel:
Nick Newall: saxophone
Gordon Edwards: piano ('Low Budget')
Producer: Raymond Douglas Davies
Running time: 43:16
Recorded at Konk Studios, London (January 1979) ('Pressure', '(Wish I Could Fly Like) Superman', 'Low Budget'); The Power Station, New York (May 1979); vocals recorded at Blue Rock Studios, New York (June 1979)
Original UK label and catalogue number: Arista Records SPART 1009
Release dates: UK: 7 September 1979, US: 10 July 1979
Chart positions: UK: –, US: 11, Australia: 79

By the time *Low Budget* was released, the UK was in the throes of a full-on mod and ska revival, with bands like Madness, The Specials and The Jam all making inroads into the charts. The Jam, in particular, would pick up on the Kinks influence, scoring a hit with 'David Watts' in August 1978. Jam leader Paul Weller has always made no secret of the fact that Ray Davies was a major influence on his songwriting. Also, the debut album of a new up-and-coming American band called Van Halen included a blistering version of 'You Really Got Me', which made people sit up and take notice of the new California-based band. Christian Nesmith – the producer son of The Monkees' Mike Nesmith – told me, 'I'd always been a fan of The Kinks. But when Van Halen released their version of 'You Really Got Me', well, it just blew me away'.

Ray wanted to build on the renewed success of the band's music, and again the songs for the new album were short, punchy, and full of insight and wit. The decision was made to record most of the album in New York rather than at Konk Studios: recording between 10 a.m. and 6 p.m. each day. This would mean they had no temptation to be indulgent and had to be a lot quicker – the result being, according to Dave Davies, that 'We did the backtracks in ten days'.

There had also been a change to the band lineup, as Jim Rodford – who joined for touring – had become a full-time member. James Walter Rodford was born in St. Albans, Hertfordshire, on 7 July 1941, and was a very experienced musician, having been in The Mike Cotton Sound and Argent (as previously mentioned). He could play bass with the best of them, and as an added bonus, he had a great voice. He slotted into The Kinks easily and remained with them until 1996, when the band went on hiatus (which has now lasted 25 years!).

Another change was with the keyboards, as Gordon Edwards had proven to be unreliable, and after failing to turn up for recording sessions, he was sacked.

All the keyboard parts on *Low Budget* (except for the piano on the title track, which was done by Edwards) were played by Ray, as the band reverted back to being a quartet.

The stalwart Nick Newell returned to play saxophone on 'Catch Me Now I'm Falling' and 'Little Bit Of Emotion', but this would be the last Kinks album he'd play on (although he would return as an additional keyboard player for the live album *One For The Road*).

The three tracks recorded at Konk were initially meant to be an EP but ended up as a single (one of three released in the UK). '(Wish I Could Fly Like) Superman' b/w 'Low Budget' was a minor hit in the US, reaching 41. This was in part due to a 12" disco remix.

As well as the songs that would eventually appear on the album, others were recorded which would appear on later albums: such as 'Destroyer', 'Massive Reductions' and 'Give The People What They Want'.

Low Budget became The Kinks' highest-placed album in the US, climbing to 11. But of course, the album failed to chart in the UK, where the band were still having little success, and indeed none of the album's singles made an impression on the singles charts except for 'Superman' in America. This was despite a review in *Melody Maker* describing the album as 'actually worth spending money on'. *Low Budget* became the first Kinks album to go gold in America, with sales of over half a million.

Another upshot of the band's growing American success was that the audience sizes increased. Up to this point in America, they'd been playing venues with capacities of 3,000 to 5,000. But from this point on – and for the next few years – they'd be playing to audiences twice that size; with a new keyboard player, about whom, more later.

The album cover was Ray's concept, with photography by Gary Gross and art direction by Ron Kellum and Donn Davenport. The front cover showed the feet of a girl wearing red shoes and shiny leggings, with two cigarette ends on the ground. The album title and name are stencilled on the ground, much like a road marking. The back cover is a letter shot, with the girl gone, but a third cigarette end in the gutter. The block design of the band name became an unofficial Kinks logo.

It's worth noting that Ray had now stopped looking back, and his more whimsical and nostalgic songs had been replaced by harder rock songs with contemporary subjects. As Mick Avory commented, 'Ray's writing was (previously) too subtle. When we did the big arenas in the late '70s, he was writing harder stuff that would come across'.

'Attitude' (Davies)

One of the last songs recorded for the album, and Ray at his angry best. It's a really strong opening, and is almost a punk song in its energy and anger. Ray is telling us he has to keep changing and updating, as he laments, 'The '80s are here/I know 'cause I'm staring right at them/But you're still waiting for 1960 to happen'. All this is disguised in a general order to change our attitude and embrace changes.

'Catch Me Now I'm Falling' (Davies)

Released as a single in the US. The US influence on the world was diminishing at this point in time, with the Marvel comics hero Captain America being a symbol of the country, and this song is about the fact that he's losing his powers and he calls for help as he has helped others in the past. Following a quiet intro and first verse with a delicate piano, we get a guitar riff similar in style to The Rolling Stones' 'Jumpin' Jack Flash'. There are multiple guitar and saxophone solos, and a far-from-plodding bass line from Jim Rodford, whose voice also adds greatly to the backing vocals throughout the album.

The song wasn't a hit, despite it being played extensively on American FM radio.

'Pressure' (Davies)

UK release: Arista Records, ARIST 321, 30 November 1979. Producer: Ray Davies. Chart positions: Did not chart

'Pressure' is another high-energy hard-rocker, with Ray venting his anger at the many sources of pressure in the world. It ends just before the two-and-a-half-minute mark, making it the album's shortest track. There's a Chuck-Berry-style guitar intro, and the song was recorded in one take with Ray 'shouting out the chords to the guys while we were doing it'.

'National Health' (Davies)

B-side to 'Pressure' in the UK.

This is similar in theme to 'Pressure', telling us that nervous tension is 'the biggest killer that's around today', and that, instead of pills, exercise is the answer. A thudding rhythm reminiscent of a heartbeat underlines the song. Ray also noodles about with a synthesizer on this one.

'(Wish I Could Fly Like) Superman' (Davies)

UK release: Arista Records, ARIST 240, 29 January 1979. Producer: Ray Davies. Chart positions: UK: –, US: 41, Australia: 71

The story behind 'Superman' is that Arista boss Clive Davis wanted a radio-and-club-friendly song, and even though Ray hated disco, he still managed to pull it off. He wrote the song after seeing *Superman: The Movie* and thinking that it was 'so true to the comic books'. The irony in the song is apparent, as the protagonist is a 'nine-stone weakling with knobbly knees' but wishes he was like Superman. But as our hero turns on the radio and hears all the bad news, he realises 'You have to be a superman to survive' and he's powerless to put right the world's ills.

'Low Budget' (Davies)
B-side to 'Superman' in the UK.

Strangely, 'Low Budget' was also the B-side to all three singles released in the US. It's sung in a London vernacular, and I have often wondered if people from other countries knew what a 'toff' was. Mind you, the full version (which isn't on the album) had a couple of extra verses which mention 'toff', 'brown ale' and 'cod roes'. Ray used to add these verses in the live shows. The lyric addresses the economic troubles of the time when the protagonist used to have expensive tastes but now has to save money. He's a 'cut-price person in a low-budget land'. In his own working-class way, Ray had always had a fear of having no money, and it has been said that this song was also a dig at the record company, as he wanted to tour, but Arista wouldn't fund it unless they had a product to promote. This resulted in the proposed EP of the three tracks recorded at Konk in January 1979 ('Low Budget', 'Superman' and 'Pressure'). It's quite a raunchy song, and it became a live favourite.

'In A Space' (Davies)
B-side to 'Moving Pictures'.

'In A Space' tells us that we are transient beings and are 'in a space/Leased by kind permission of the human race'. It's a great plodding behemoth of a song, with Ray and Dave sharing lead vocals on the chorus (with Dave a full octave higher).

'Little Bit Of Emotion' (Davies)
An intricate and lovely little song, reminding us that keeping our feelings bottled up doesn't help, and that we should let our feelings show. The first part of the final verse is backed by the bass synth, which is really effective.

'A Gallon Of Gas' (Davies)
Released as a single in America and Japan and was the B-side to 'Pressure' in France. This is another song addressing the economic problems of the time. In America, the problems hit the average US man where it hurt: his car. It also suggests that it's easier to buy drugs than gasoline. It's a bluesy arrangement, and I think that any other treatment would've ruined the song.

'Misery' (Davies)
Ray is addressing all the miserable people, telling them to cheer up because 'Until you learn to laugh/You'll never come to any parties at my house'. It's a mid-tempo rocker that wouldn't have been out of place on the *Schoolboys In Disgrace* album.

'Moving Pictures' (Davies)
UK release: Arista Records, ARIST 300, 28 September 1979. Producer: Ray Davies. Chart positions: Did not chart

'Moving Pictures' comments on how life just passes us by, using the line 'Nothing in life is a permanent fixture', just like a movie. It has a slight disco feel, and the lyric mentions racial problems: 'Black girls, white girls, oh what a mixture/Looking as pretty as a picture'.

Bonus Tracks from the 1998 reissue on Konk/Velvel (63467-79727-2)

'A Gallon Of Gas' (US single extended edit) (Davies)
An extended version (by one second?!) of the US album track.

'Catch Me Now I'm Falling' (Extended edit) (Davies)
The extension for the US single was 49 seconds.

'(Wish I Could Fly Like) Superman' (Disco mix) (Davies)
This version is two and a half minutes longer than the album track and was seemingly influenced by Blondie's success with 'Heart Of Glass'. The track was edited and remixed at Konk Studios and issued in January 1979, and it proved to be a great disco song, as Ray explained: 'I had to produce a little bit. I really got it to be a good dance record on the remix. The proof was when I was in a discotheque in Stockholm, where all they play is disco music. It came on, and it knocked the balls off everything else'.

One For The Road (1980)

Personnel:
Ray Davies: vocals, guitar, harmonica, keyboards
Dave Davies: lead guitar, backing vocals
Jim Rodford: bass, backing vocals
Mick Avory: drums
Ian Gibbons: keyboards, backing vocals
Additional personnel:
Nick Newall: keyboards
Producer: Raymond Douglas Davies
Running time: 77:21
Recorded at various concerts in the US and Switzerland in 1979/1980; Overdubs at Konk Studios, London, and Blue Rock Studios, New York in November/December 1979 and March 1980.
Release dates: UK: 1 August 1980, US: 4 June 1980
Original UK label and catalogue number: Arista Records DARTY 6
Chart positions: UK: –, US: 14, Australia: 71
Tracklisting: 'Opening' (Davies), 'The Hard Way' (Davies), 'Catch Me Now I'm Falling' (Davies), 'Where Have All The Good Times Gone' (Davies), 'Intro: Lola' (Davies), 'Lola' (Davies), 'Pressure' (Davies), 'All Day And All Of The Night' (Davies), '20th Century Man' (Davies), 'Misfits' (Davies), 'Prince Of The Punks' (Davies), 'Low Budget' (Davies), 'Attitude' (Davies), '(Wish I Could Fly Like) Superman' (Davies), 'National Health' (Davies), 'Till The End Of The Day' (Davies), 'Celluloid Heroes' (Davies), 'You Really Got Me' (Davies), 'Victoria' (Davies), 'David Watts' (Davies)

The re-energised Kinks toured America relentlessly throughout 1979 and 1980. In fact, they toured the States every single year of the 1970s and 1980s, with the exception of 1986. But for the dates promoting the *Low Budget* album, they needed to find a new keyboard player, and they found him in the form of Ian Gibbons.

Ian was born on 18 July 1952 and began playing the accordion at the age of nine. He later played guitar in a rock band he formed at school before taking up the organ upon leaving. He played with a number of bands throughout the 1970s, including Love Affair and The Nashville Teens, and in early 1979 was asked to audition for The Kinks. Ian said: Jim (Rodford) phoned me up, as I'd previously done session work with him. I did an audition while Ray was mixing *Low Budget*. On the first day, I went up into the piano booth with Mick, Jim and Dave, and Ray popped his head in'. Ian's affable demeanour and obvious skills as a keyboard player and singer were not lost on Ray, as he relates: 'I walked into the piano booth where Ian was singing 'Let It Be', and the rest of the band were joining in. I thought Ian was cheeky enough to get the gig'. After three or four days of rehearsal, the band travelled to America for the tour, with the five-piece band and additional keyboard player Nick Newall.

Ray had been toying with the idea of making *Low Budget* a half-studio/half-live album like *Everybody's In Showbiz*, but the idea was discarded. But he had many concerts recorded for a live album, and tapes were sent over to Konk Studios engineer John Rollo: 'They'd ship the tapes back to me, and what I'd try to do was find the best performances of each song from about 30 or 40 shows'. The end result was a double live album titled *One For The Road,* which was issued in America in June 1980, with the British release coming in August. This was a different band than the one that recorded *Kelvin Hall* and the live half of *Everybody's In Showbiz.* Where the audience was an integral part of the first and – to a slightly lesser extent – the second, the audience sizes were much bigger this time around, as were the venue sizes. As such, the band were more distant but still put in amazing performances.

The material was much more in keeping with their current status as a successful rock band. It was harder, more punchy, and with more than a nod to the punk scene. No less than eight of the 19 songs came from *Misfits* and *Low Budget*, with the punky *Prince Of The Punks* thrown in. The others appeared to be the ones that resonated with the younger audiences who were getting to hear the band through the new mod revival – mod anthems if you like, plus live favourites such as 'Lola', 'The Hard Way' and 'Celluloid Heroes', the last of which giving some respite from the harder rock of the present-day Kinks. There was none of the wistful Englishness, as songs like 'Sunny Afternoon' and 'Waterloo Sunset' were omitted.

Jim Rodford's bass skills were having a positive effect on the band, as he helped keep Mick Avory sharp, thereby negating the complaints that Dave Davies seemed to have with the drummer. But the American-style rock The Kinks were now playing didn't help their UK sales, as this music was a bit out of fashion in their homeland and wouldn't take off for another couple of years (the band being a sort of trendsetter and years ahead of its time). The album's success in America could've been due to the reception at the venues, most of which were in the North-Eastern states. The Kinks had always done well in the 13 original colonies.

The advances in recording equipment resulted in overall excellent sound quality on the album, and with much better and experienced musicianship, far better than had gone before. Sadly, the critics were not impressed, with one calling it 'a reason for live albums to be banned'.

A new format was beginning to rear its head around this time: home video. Ray thought (correctly) that this was the future, and a 60-minute version of the album was released on videocassette in the US on 25 June 1980. (The DVD was released in 2006.)

The album cover was mainly magenta, with a photograph of Ray on the front and Dave on the back. Yellow stripes containing the band name and album title as a ticker-tape also adorned the cover. The photography was by Lauren Recht, with art direction by Howard Fritzson. Two singles were released in America – 'Lola' b/w 'Celluloid Heroes' on 23 July 1980, and 'You Really Got

Me' b/w 'Attitude' on 29 October 1980, but neither release troubled the charts. No singles were issued in the UK, but the 1981 single 'Better Things' (from *Give The People What They Want*) was issued with a bonus single of 'Lola' b/w 'David Watts' from *One For The Road*.

Give The People What They Want (1981)

Personnel:
Ray Davies: vocals, guitar, keyboards
Dave Davies: lead guitar, vocals
Jim Rodford: bass
Mick Avory: drums
Ian Gibbons: keyboards
Additional personnel:
Chrissie Hynde: uncredited backing vocals ('Predictable', 'Add It Up', 'Art Lover', 'A Little Bit Of Abuse')
Producer: Raymond Douglas Davies
Running time: 41:09
Recorded at Konk Studios, London (June 1980, April-June 1981)
Release dates: UK: 15 January 1982, US: 26 August 1981
Original UK label and catalogue number: Arista Records SPART 1171
Chart positions: UK: –, US: 15

The Kinks were back at Konk Studios in the spring of 1981 (after some work the previous June) recording their 19th studio album, and for the first time in a while the lineup was unchanged from the last album: a stable band at last. (There were a few additional vocals from Chrissie Hynde of The Pretenders, but we were unaware of this at the time.)

In June 1981, Dave released his second solo album – *Glamour* – but frustratingly for him it failed to sell, reaching only 152 in America.

Give The People What They Want was not just the title of the new Kinks album but was also a statement of intent. The upsurge in the band's popularity seemed to be aligned with the fact that they were now a harder rock band and no longer the makers of nostalgic records, nor the theatrical showmen (although Ray was becoming a more forceful frontman with his red jackets, bow-ties and stage antics) of the 1960s and early 1970s. The album's eleven tracks were mainly out-and-out rock songs full of power chords and perfect for their American audiences. Ray's original plan was for the album to be a statement about the media, but there seemed to be no real overall theme, as he gave us songs about murderers ('Killer's Eyes'), voyeurs ('Art Lover'), domestic violence ('A Little Bit Of Abuse') and a wife/husband role reversal ('Yo-Yo').

The tours of America in 1981 featured songs from the new album but were notable for a couple of special events. Firstly, at their Toronto show on 25 September 1981, they were joined on stage by Pete Quaife, who was living in Canada at the time. This was the first time the four original Kinks members had shared a stage in twelve years. They performed the Chuck Berry song 'Little Queenie'. But Pete later admitted that he was so drunk (due to a roadie giving him a glass of vodka instead of water), he remembered very little of it, and when he went back on stage to do an encore, 'Dave kept yelling at me, telling me I was playing in the wrong key'.

The second event was on 3 October 1981, when the band played New York's Madison Square Garden for the first time. Ray and Dave fulfilled a promise, flying their widowed mother over to see the show.

The album's harder sound was a deliberate attempt to pander to the arena rock fans in the States, and also managed to satisfy Ray Davies' songwriting goals. The album's 41 minutes and nine seconds all contain his sardonic humour and scathing pronouncements.

After the album's American release in August, Ray held back the British release until the following January because he wanted to produce a full-length video of the album, and also remix it for European release. Sadly, the financing for the projects fell through. But a video was produced for 'Predictable'. It was directed by Julien Temple (who would direct future Kinks' promo films) and was very well-received, getting almost saturation play on MTV. This was almost certainly a Ray-only project, as Dave has said that he didn't know about it until it was broadcast, but he thought it was funny.

The album's front cover has a photograph of Ray running past Konk Studios after apparently spraying the album title on the wall. The photo has a grey surround with the band name in red, in a scrawl similar to that on *Sleepwalker* and *Misfits* – not really surprising, as the lettering was again by Hal Fiedler. The cover photographs were taken by Robert Ellis, and art direction was by Neal Pozner. The back cover has a photograph of a sheet of corrugated iron with the album title and band name, a grey surround and a tracklist. Corrugated iron would have a bearing on the sound of some of the tracks, as we shall see.

The album title was prophetic, as it was indeed what the people wanted, in America anyway, as it climbed to 15 in the charts there – making it a hat-trick of top-20 albums – and also went gold. Naturally, the UK didn't agree, and it didn't chart. The American sales no doubt were helped by the band touring there throughout 1980 and 1981 (although I know they toured the UK at least twice in those years 'cos I was there). Any one of the 11 tracks could've been released as a single, and in fact, two were released in the UK: 'Better Things' and 'Predictable'. Two singles were also released in the US: 'Destroyer' and 'Better Things'.

'Around The Dial' (Davies)
The radio-static intro was used as the intro to shows at the time and, along with the title track, announced The Kinks as a band on the fringe of metal. But it has a serious lyric about the changes that happen in the media: one minute you're all over the place, and then you've been forgotten. Ray fashioned this message into a lament that his favourite DJ has been taken off the air as he's now fallen out of favour with the masses. Ray likens it to The Kinks' previous disappearance from the airwaves, asking, 'Are you listening to me?' and 'Can you hear me?'.

'Give The People What They Want' (Davies)
This was originally recorded for and supposed to be on the *Low Budget* album but was held back. This rocker is Ray's ironic comment on how the mass media

operate. You have to 'give the people what they want', but 'The more they get, the more they need'.

'Killer's Eyes' (Davies)
This was about the Turkish Mehmet Ali Agca's attempt to assassinate Pope John Paul II on 13 May 1981. What is in the mind of someone who could do that? Ray tries to look behind the killer's eyes in this slower, slightly sinister-sounding song. Although Ali Agca was sentenced to life imprisonment, the Pope forgave him, and Agca was pardoned by the Italian President (at the Pope's request) and deported to his native Turkey in June 2000. Ironically, he later converted to Roman Catholicism.

'Predictable' (Davies)
UK release: Arista Records, ARIST 426, 30 October 1981. Producer: Ray Davies. Chart positions: UK: –, US: 81, Australia: 97
'Predictable' is about the monotony of the average person's life, and to some extent, depression. Ray sings, 'Ain't life a bore' and 'It feels like a good time to die'. However, there is some hope, as he also says, 'One day it's gonna get better some way'. It has a great video with Ray on his own, dressing in different styles from the 1930s to the 1980s. Despite the lyric content, the song has a superb pounding rhythm.

'Add It Up' (Davies)
This is about someone's rise to success. At first, you're waiting in line for a bus, but now you drive around in a limousine. You have all the trappings of wealth (Ray mentions Gucci and Cartier), but then we get the Ray Davies sting: you're lonely and you're getting older. It's a fast song, in keeping with the album's overall sonic feel. The refrain of 'Add it up' is very like punk rock band The Damned's 'Smash It Up' from 1979.

'Destroyer' (Davies)
US single A-side.
This reached 80 in the *Billboard* charts and three on the mainstream radio charts. It was also a moderate hit in Canada, getting to 35. It's another rocker from the *Low Budget* sessions. It references the band's history by using the riff from 'All Day And All Of The Night' and name-checking 'Lola'. The song is a warning that creativity comes at a price: to create something means you have to destroy a bit of yourself.

'Yo-Yo' (Davies)
B-side to 'Better Things' in the US. The subject matter is a woman's role in a man's life. The first part of the song has the woman being the dutiful wife at home while the man works. Then *she* goes out to work and we approach that

aspect from the man's point of view. It contains a Ray line that sums the man up: 'I don't fit in, but I don't stand out'. This song gave us a breather from the fast pace of the previous tracks.

Here is where the aforementioned corrugated iron comes in, as, on this song and the previous one, the band wanted a really hard drum sound. Drummer Mick Avory recalled: 'We knew a builder down the road, and we got hold of some of that way – corrugated iron that was used to make air raid shelters. We lined the studio with it when we recorded the drums'.

'Back To Front' (Davies)
B-side to 'Predictable' in the UK. Also the B-side to 'Destroyer' in America. This has contradictory lyrics, as Ray looks back and realises that all his friends now have different views to him, and his life is indeed back-to-front from everybody else. This heavier song ends with him shouting to the band that they 'have to do it all over again', as it's his view (and what he wants) that matters.

'Art Lover' (Davies)
This second slower song appears to be about a person who watches the children playing in a park. Ray says he used to take his own children to the park and watch the others playing. But are you relishing the art of beautiful bodies (remember that many religious paintings have naked children in them), or are you watching them for other – less honourable reasons? There is a sinister part where Ray sings, 'Come to Daddy and I'll give you some Spangles'. Would Americans know what Spangles were? Even though they were advertised by William Boyd (TV's Hopalong Cassidy), Spangles (a flavoured boiled sweet) were only available in Britain from 1950 to 1985 and then briefly in 1995.

'A Little Bit Of Abuse' (Davies)
This one is about domestic violence. Ray somehow manages to inject a little humour into this mid-tempo song, with the line 'Excuse me, is this your tooth?'. He makes a very serious point that many sufferers of domestic violence stay with the abusive partner and make excuses about their injuries.

'Better Things' (Davies)
UK release: Arista Records, ARIST 415, 19 June 1981. Producer: Ray Davies. Chart positions: UK: 46, US: 92, Australia: –
'Better Things' was a UK and US single A-side. It reached 46 in the UK, 92 on the US *Billboard* chart and 12 on the mainstream radio chart. It was the first Kinks single in the British charts since 'Supersonic Rocket Ship' in 1972. The single is 15 seconds longer than the album version. It was written about the breakdown of Ray's second marriage (to Yvonne), but is an upbeat song, with him saying, 'I know tomorrow you'll find better things'. An early version of the song was attempted during the *Low Budget* sessions. When released as a

single in the UK, a free bonus single was included containing live versions of 'Lola' and 'David Watts (from the *One For The Road* album), with the catalogue number KINKS 1.

State Of Confusion (1983)

Personnel:
Ray Davies: lead vocals, rhythm guitar, synthesizer, piano
Dave Davies: lead guitar, vocals
Jim Rodford: bass
Mick Avory: drums
Ian Gibbons: keyboards
Additional personnel:
John Beecham: trombone ('Come Dancing')
Noel Morris: trumpet ('Come Dancing')
Andy Hamilton: tenor saxophone ('Come Dancing')
Alan Holmes: baritone saxophone ('Come Dancing')
Kate Williams" spoken voice ('Come Dancing')
Producer: Raymond Douglas Davies
Running time: 41:20
Recorded at Konk Studios, London (May/June 1981; October 1982 to March 1983)
Release dates: UK: 10 June 1983, US: 24 May 1983
Original UK label and catalogue number: Arista Records 205 275
Chart positions: UK: –, US: 12, Australia: 96

One of the tracks for the next Kinks album had already been recorded when the band reconvened at Konk Studios in October 1982, and that was Dave Davies' sole song on the album: 'Bernadette'. The lineup was unchanged, although, as usual, all was not well between Ray and Dave, and indeed Dave and Mick. This resulted in the album being recorded in stages. Jim Rodford, Ray and Mick recorded the basic tracks together, then Ian Gibbons added his keyboard parts, and finally, Dave recorded his guitar parts alone.

The band was still touring heavily, which was another problem for Mick – as we shall see later – and the onstage altercations between him and Dave were not showing any signs of abating. On one particular occasion at Long Island's Nassau Coliseum, Mick kicked over his drums and left the stage, refusing to share a stage with the younger Davies. Ray told the audience that Mick had been called away for an important phone call before going backstage and persuading the seething drummer to return. Apparently, Mick said, 'I'll do it for you', to which Ray said, 'What about the 14,000 people?'. Mick replied, 'Okay, I'll do it for them as well'. After the show, Ray threw a plate of curry at Dave.

Dave had always seemed to have a problem with Mick's drumming, but the main thing that galled him was that, as one-third of The Kinks' directorship, Mick was often caught in the middle of discussions (some may say arguments) between Ray and Dave over band policy and decision-making. Dave complained that Mick either sided with Ray or stayed neutral, which of course, meant the discussions went on for longer than they should. Dave thought that Mick was siding with Ray and never with him; Mick was keeping himself in a job.

Following the completion of the album, Dave was also upset at Ray. Dave had been feeling put out by the lack of credit he received for the work he was putting in on song arrangements, so he went through all the liner notes and credits for the album, making sure he had his just dues. However, when the album was released, he discovered that his name wasn't there (apart from his playing and composer credits). He later claimed in his autobiography that Ray had telephoned Arista the night before the album cover was due to be printed and made a final set of changes, removing Dave's credits.

The album was preceded by the single 'Come Dancing', which proved to be one of Ray's best decisions, as Clive Davis at Arista wanted the track 'Don't Forget To Dance' to be the lead single. Initially released in November 1982 in the UK, 'Come Dancing' initially failed to sell. But then the video – again directed by Julien Temple – began to get extensive airplay on MTV, and upon release in the US in April, the song rocketed to number 6, equalling their highest-ever US chart placing: 'Tired Of Waiting For You'. Jonathan King featured the single in a segment on the BBC's flagship music show *Top Of The Pops*, and the interest resulted in the single being re-released in Britain. As well as showing the video, the band also *appeared* on the show, and the single was their biggest UK hit since 'Apeman' in 1970: reaching the lofty height of number 12. The *Top Of The Pops* appearance – recorded and broadcast on 24 August 1983 – was unusual, as Dave wasn't there. He'd been called away to record a video for his third solo album *Chosen People*, which was released in August.

The album cover was very similar to *Give The People What They Want*, with the wall outside Konk Studios and the album title scrawled on it (Not really; the words were added by the artist). The photograph also has all of the band and not just Ray running away. The surround is very 1980s, with purple, yellow, green and white, and the band name and album title again: in differing lettering styles (maybe denoting a 'state of confusion'). The back cover has the same colours with a band portrait (all band members appearing to look in different directions: again probably denoting confusion) and a tracklist. The cover's art direction was by Howard Fritzson, with photography by Robert Ellis.

The album's sound was similar to that of the previous one, as all tracks are short, punchy, rocky, and above all, radio-and-arena-rock-friendly. But strangely, the two tracks singles were probably the least representative of the album's hard sound.

State Of Confusion was another successful album in America, reaching 12 in the charts, and was certified Gold in Canada. A cassette version was also issued with an extra track tagged on the end of each side ('Noise' and 'Long Distance'). Whilst not charting in Britain (what a surprise, NOT!), the album reached 96 in Australia and 55 in Germany. Two singles were released in the UK, and amazingly, both were hits. And though The Kinks would have two more UK chart entries in the ensuing years, neither of them could really be classed as hits, so these two – 'Come Dancing' and 'Don't Forget To Dance' – were their last hits in their homeland.

Before the band's next album, there were changes in the air. But they had by now recorded a grand total of 20 – repeat, 20 – studio albums. How many bands can say that?

'State Of Confusion' (Davies)

This was released as a single in continental Europe, but not in America, though it reached 26 on *Billboard*'s Hot Mainstream Rock Tracks chart. This song replaced what was meant to be the album's title track – a song called 'Entertainment', which wouldn't see release until the 1989 album *UK Jive*. The angst-filled scream at the start suggests true anger, but two musical bridges suggest different moods. Ray's lyric shows various sources of frustration: technological failures, domestic problems, and even just crossing the road. In the end, he concludes that there is 'no escape from the state of confusion I'm in'. A video (again directed by Julien Temple) accompanied this track.

'Definite Maybe' (Davies)

Ray has another bout of spleen-venting here as he rails against bureaucracy, and when he tries to put things right, he gets tied up in more red tape, as he says, 'All I ever get is a definite maybe'. This track is featured on the inner sleeve, with a band portrait with 'definite' and 'maybe?' being the thoughts of Mick and Dave, and Ian and Jim saying, 'No decision, no decision'. Despite the frustration, it's a great up-tempo pop song.

'Labour Of Love' (Davies)

B-side to 'State Of Confusion' in Europe. Mr. and Mrs. Horrible have been married for years, and they think they're just staying together as a 'labour of love'; one 'head' wants to do one thing, and the other, another. However, in the end, they realise they can't live without each other. The intro invokes the 'Wedding March', given a Jimi Hendrix treatment by Dave. This one is a mid-tempo rock song that *must* have gone down well live.

'Come Dancing' (Davies)

UK release: Arista Records, ARIST 502, 19 November 1982, 21 April 1983 (US). Producer: Ray Davies. Chart positions: UK: 12, US: 6, Australia: 36

'Come Dancing' received an award from ASCAP (American Society of Composers, Authors and Publishers) on 27 October 1983 as one of the most played songs Of 1983'. It reached six in Canada and on *Billboard*'s Hot 100, four in Ireland, and was top 30 in Belgium, Switzerland and the Netherlands, proving that Ray's choice of single was better than what the record company wanted. He brought out the brass section for this one but tweaked it to sound more like a big band, in keeping with the song. And as an added bonus, when the song develops a more modern style later in the song, we get a riff based on 'You Really Got Me'.

The song is about Ray and Dave's sister Rene, who used to go out dancing at the local dance hall. In fact, on Ray's 13th birthday, Rene gave him a guitar before going out dancing. Sadly, she had a weak heart and died that same night. It also mirrors Lionel Bart's 'Fings Ain't Wot They Used To Be'. The 'Come Dancing' lyric states 'Before that they put up a bowling alley/On the site that used to be the local palais', whereas Bart's lyric says 'They've changed our local palais into a bowling alley'.

The song has a great Julien Temple video, which faithfully tells the story with Ray as a spiv. It's a very English song, and Ray has stated that he aimed it at the band's dwindling British audience. The video was filmed in November 1982 at the Ilford Palais, which, ironically, was demolished in 2007 to make way for some flats.

In keeping with the trends of the time, this was The Kinks' second single to be released as a 12" extended remix version.

'Property' (Davies)
There is vocoder on this one, which appears to be about a relationship breakup, with one partner moving out, but they have no plans. This slower track is rather wistful and somewhat sad, as the two people in the song divide up their property.

'Don't Forget To Dance' (Davies)
UK release: Arista Records, ARIST 524, 30 September 1983, 1 August 1983 (US). Producer: Ray Davies. Chart positions: UK: 58, US: 29, Australia: –
This A-side was originally recorded at Grand Slam Studios in New Jersey and then at Konk. It climbed to 29 on *Billboard*'s Hot 100, 16 on their Mainstream Rock chart, 23 on their Adult Contemporary chart, and reached 20 in Canada and 38 in New Zealand.

A lonely middle-aged woman thinks she's missed her chance for happiness, but Ray tells her to cheer up and 'Don't forget to dance'. The song is a ballad and continues the sad theme from the previous track. The promotional video has the spiv again: a character Ray based on his Uncle Frankie.

'Young Conservatives' (Davies)
B-side to 'Don't Forget To Dance' in the US. Ray is commenting on class again, with what could be a sequel to 'A Well Respected Man'. It might also be about the adult version of 'David Watts' – in fact, the song does have tonal similarities to it, with a nod to the 'fa, fa, fa' about halfway through and at the end.

'Heart Of Gold' (Davies)
The guitars have less of a crunch and more of a jangle on this acoustic (and almost country) ballad that sounds not a million miles away from The Pretenders. In fact, Ray said this song was inspired by the January 1983 birth of his and Chrissie Hynde's daughter Natalie. Hidden in the song are some

allusions to sibling rivalry (Who could he be talking about?), and he uses his gift of melody to smuggle in incisive lyrics. Dave joins in the chorus with his trademark vocals, an octave higher than Ray.

'Cliches Of The World (B Movie)' (Davies)
One of Ray's forays into political comment. He's concerned at the state of his home country, and the protagonist is 'disillusioned at the promises' the politicians made. It's a comment on the failure of socialism in post-war Britain (We were in the 1980s: the Thatcher years). Crunching heavy metal guitar opens the song, which is one of Ray's most vitriolic, as he almost spits the words out (except the spoken section).

'Bernadette' (Davies)
B-side to 'Don't Forget To Dance'.
Dave channels his inner Little Richard in this screamer about the gold-digging Bernadette. The singer doesn't want to leave her, but as he sings, 'You are so expensive/You've never done a day's work in your life'.

Bonus Tracks from the 1999 reissue on Konk/Velvel (63467-79731-2)
'Don't Forget To Dance' (Original extended edit) (Davies)
The 12" version is about half a minute longer than the album version. This track, along with the next one, remained unreleased until the 1999 Velvel reissue.

'Once A Thief' (Davies)
The protagonist was a thief and was being shunned, but someone took him in. However, he feels as though he's not trusted: 'Once a thief, always a suspect', he sings. This would not have been out of place on the album. It's a good mid-tempo pop/rock song.

'Long Distance' (Davies)
This lyric seems to be about touring in Australia – 'Damn hotel is feeling like a cell', 'Trying to keep my head together/In that hot Australia weather'. All he wants, is to ring long-distance and talk to home. It's a country song that takes us back to *Muswell Hillbillies*. This track was previously only available on the album's cassette version.

'Noise' (Davies)
B-side to 'Come Dancing'.
This is a slow rocker in which Ray indulges his penchant for writing about things that annoyed him. Mick Avory said, 'Perhaps you wanna lay in 'cause you got the flu, and you get woken up by builders digging the road up somewhere with a pneumatic drill or a jackhammer. So, there is a sense of humour in it'.

Word Of Mouth (1984)

Personnel:
Ray Davies: vocals, guitar, keyboards, harmonica, drum machine ('Good Day', 'Do It Again', 'Living On A Thin Line')
Dave Davies: lead guitar, vocals
Jim Rodford: bass, backing vocals
Mick Avory: drums, percussion ('Missing Persons', 'Sold Me Out', 'Going Solo')
Ian Gibbons: keyboards, backing vocals
Bob Henrit: drums, percussion ('Word Of Mouth', 'Massive Reductions', Guilty', 'Too Hot', 'Summer's Gone')
Producer: Raymond Douglas Davies
Associate producer: Dave Davies
Running time: 43:04
Recorded at Konk Studios, London (June/July 1983; June, August and September 1984)
Release date: 19 November 1984
Original UK label and catalogue number: Arista Records 206 685
Chart positions: UK: –, US: 57

The band had started recording sessions for *Word Of Mouth* in mid-1983 and put down three tracks. But due to touring and other commitments, they couldn't carry on until a year later. In that time, many things happened in the Kinks' kamp (Sorry, I couldn't resist that one).

Ray was working on a project for Channel 4: a short film called *Return To Waterloo*. The 57-minute film stars Ken Colley as The Traveller, who is commuting from Guildford to Waterloo on the train. But in a typical Ray Davies twist, a darker image – that he might be a serial rapist – is inferred. Also in the cast is a young Tim Roth, and Dominique Barnes, who'd played the daughter in the television adaptation of Hunter Davies' (no relation) *Punch* column *Father's Day*. Ray also puts in an appearance as a subway busker – a character that would reappear in the video for the forthcoming single 'Do It Again'.

The story isn't told through spoken word but through song (Does that make it an opera then?), with nine songs being recorded for the soundtrack. The music was recorded by Ray, Mick Avory, Ian Gibbons and Jim Rodford. Dave declined to take part as, at the time, he thought Ray was spending too much time on that project rather than concentrating on Kinks work. Dave was also miffed that his solo album *Chosen People* hadn't had the success he hoped for (We wouldn't see another Dave Davies solo album until 2002). However, he thought that the finished film was a good one. With Dave not taking part, it was decided that the soundtrack did not qualify as a Kinks album, so when it was released early in 1985, it was classed as a Ray Davies solo album: his first. Dave was so disenchanted that he refused to take part in the band's American tour to promote the *State Of Confusion* album, which was subsequently cancelled. This infuriated Ray, and Dave now says that this decision was 'foolish'.

Rather-more-important events took place during the period between recording sessions. On a personal level, Ray and Chrissie's relationship broke down, and early in 1984, she left him, taking Natalie with her. She married Simple Minds' leader Jim Kerr in the May. Also, after years of disagreements and physical incidents, Mick Avory made the decision to leave The Kinks. Some sources state he was sacked by Dave, and others state Ray took him out for a drink to discuss the matter. Apparently, Mick was fed up with all the arguments. And with Ray saying that if they did another album, there would be more touring, Mick made the difficult decision to leave the band. He played his last Kinks show in Leicester in April 1984 – a month before they were due to go back into the studio to continue work on the new album. Though Mick was no longer in the band, he continued working at Konk in an administrative role. He would also appear on subsequent albums – the only one he didn't appear on was the final one *Phobia*.

Mick's replacement was seasoned skinsman Bob Henrit. Not only had Bob played on Dave's solo albums, but in the first half of the 1970s, he was with Jim Rodford in the band Argent, so their past working relationship provided a continuity to The Kinks rhythm section. Bob – born in the Hertfordshire town of Broxbourne on 2 May 1944 – had played with Adam Faith's backing band The Roulettes, and Unit 4 + 2, who had a 1965 hit with 'Concrete And Clay', on which Bob had drummed as a session player. After being in Argent throughout their existence, he played in the band Charlie, who had opened for The Kinks on their 1978 tour.

Word Of Mouth contained 11 songs, nine of which were written by Ray and two by Dave. Three of them – 'Sold Me Out', 'Missing Persons' and 'Going Solo' – were reworked songs from the *Return To Waterloo* project. There are a couple of possible reasons for this. Perhaps Ray's writing had been affected adversely by the fallout from the breakup with Chrissie Hynde, or he might've thought the songs were too strong to be sidelined and would be better-received on a Kinks album. Either way, they are great songs. In fact, *Word Of Mouth* contains some of Ray's more-accessible songs, as he wasn't channelling his own feelings and worries. They are more-straightforward songs, and this is probably one of the reasons why the album – even though not one of the bands' best sellers – had gained a sort of cult (should that be 'kult'?) following amongst Kinks fans. It is in equal parts a rock album and a pop album. In fact, since it was promoted poorly, the album title was rather apt, as that's how many people found out about the album.

The cover is typically 1980s, with images of lips (denoting word-of-mouth), and the band name and album title scrawled as if by lipstick. The back cover has more lips, a tracklist and some credits: which list Dave Davies as 'Associate Producer'. As with the previous album, Howard Fritzson had some artistic input by designing the logo (such as it is). The illustration was by Brooklyn artist Renate Sturmer, and the design was by Maude Gilman. The overall cover concept was by Chris Morton and art direction by Donn Davenport.

Upon release in the States, the album didn't do as well as the previous Arista albums, only getting to 57. But it did spend 20 weeks on the chart. And, no, you don't even have to ask about its performance in Britain.

Not many singles were released from this album, with only 'Do It Again' and 'Good Day' issued in Britain, and 'Summer's Gone' in America. 'Living On A Thin Line' was issued as a 12" promotional disc for radio stations in the US.

'Do It Again' (Davies)

UK release: Arista Records, ARIST 617, 4 December 1984. Producer: Ray Davies. Chart positions: UK: –, US: 41, Australia: –

The opening guitar chord of 'Do It Again' is reminiscent of The Beatles' 'A Hard Day's Night'. Then it launches into one of the best classic rock songs the band ever recorded. It was also released as a single in America, where it reached 41 (4 on the Mainstream Rock Tracks chart). It also reached 91 in Canada. With a drum machine also on this one, I assume this and the two other tracks with a drum machine were recorded in the gap between Mick Avory leaving and Bob Henrit joining. Dave has some soaring guitar solos.

The song was used in the 2006 film *Click*, and in TV promotion for the 2013 Tour De France. Ray says the song is about stressful work schedules: 'I think it applies to everybody who gets up in the morning and has to go out and do their job'. The video by Julien Temple had both Ray and Mick Avory as buskers. Ray insisted that Mick Avory appear in the video, even though he didn't play on the track: showing that Ray bore the drummer no ill feelings.

'Word Of Mouth' (Davies)

Another out-and-out 1980s-style rock song, which has Ray (and Dave an octave higher) saying that even though all the telephone boxes have been vandalised, news will always get through: usually by 'word of mouth'.

'Good Day' (Davies)

UK release: Arista Records, ARIST 577, 10 August 1984. Producer: Ray Davies. Chart positions: UK: –, US: 81, Australia: 97

On 'Good Day', a drum machine was used instead of a drummer. The song opens with an alarm clock, which grabs our attention, but in keeping with Ray putting in his own twist, the alarm is an electronic beeping one, which were just becoming popular. Lyrically, despite all the bad news, today 'had better be a good day'. This mid-tempo pop song name-checks English actress and sex-siren Diana Dors, who died in May 1984. It has a great ending (extended on the 12" version) with pealing bells.

'Living On A Thin Line' (Dave Davies)

This was released as a radio promo single in the US. Dave has stated that it's about his personal hatred of politicians and also the deterioration of

Englishness. 'There's no England now', he laments, and wants to return to the 'days of old'. Swirling Pink-Floyd-style synthesizers underline this great song. The promo record released in America was on 12" vinyl and got to 24 on the Mainstream Rock Tracks chart. Also recorded with a drum machine, Dave wrote it for Ray to sing, but Ray wasn't keen, so Dave sang it. But he'd written it for Ray's voice, 'So I had to try and sing it in a low register'.

It was used three times in the 2001 'University' episode of *The Sopranos* TV series, and according to the show's producer Terence Winter, it is the series' most asked-about song.

This song was another reason for the added tension between the Davies brothers. Dave looked into why – after all the airplay it received in America – it wasn't released as a single. It transpired that Ray had a deal with the record company that the first three singles from any album would be songs written by him – and there aren't many albums that have four singles.

'Sold Me Out' (Davies)
B-side to the 'Living On The Thin Line' promo in America. This was a particular favourite of Dave's from *Return To Waterloo*. Having not appeared on the original soundtrack recording, he was keen to make an impact on this version, and his enthusiasm is apparent from the outset with some fantastic jangling guitar. Ray lets his paranoia out on this rocker, saying, 'You sold me out' to 'get a better deal for yourself'.

'Massive Reductions' (Davies)
A version of this was the B-side to the single 'Better Things' in 1981. This updated version has a more 1980s rock sound and begins with a trumpet and synthesiser, which is really attention-grabbing. Ray sings here about a company (the record company) making 'massive reductions to stay alive', and how his big house, car and expense account have been taken from him.

'Guilty' (Dave Davies)
Dave vents his anger and frustration with his record company – who hadn't promoted his solo album *Chosen People* well enough – and other frustrations such as those in power 'controlling the masses with your businesslike fashion'. It also addresses Dave's interest in spiritual matters, with the line 'Don't stand in the light for the truth/It will blind you'. This is a typical Dave Davies song, with crunching, no-nonsense guitar.

'Too Hot' (Davies)
This addresses the nation's obsession with keeping fit and gymnasiums – it's too hot indoors, and when you go outside, it's the height of summer and the city is also too hot. The speed of the song is like an exercise video – you can almost imagine people on their treadmills. Julien Temple gets a name-check

on this one: 'Julien is out there looking at locations'. In fact, Julien had been directing Ray in the film Absolute Beginners, where he played Patsy Kensit's father alongside another British music legend: David Bowie. Sadly, the film flopped – the budget of £8.4 million wasn't matched by the box office takings of £1.8 million.

'Missing Persons' (Davies)
A wistful track that was originally recorded for the *Return To Waterloo* film. It's a very sad song about a father's anguish at the disappearance of his daughter. At under three minutes, it's the album's shortest song.

'Summer's Gone' (Davies)
B-Side of the 12" version of 'Do It Again' in the UK.
'Summer's Gone' was released as a single in the US, but didn't chart. The single is 19 seconds shorter than the album version. It's another mid-tempo pop-rock song, looking back to a happy summer, but now 'It feels like summer's gone'. We also get some electronic thunder to illustrate the rain.

'Going Solo' (Davies)
B-side to 'Summer's Gone' in America. This is the third song Ray wrote for *Return To Waterloo* that was re-recorded for this album. The missing girl from 'Missing Persons' has actually run away and is 'going solo'. Despite the lyrics, this is quite a jaunty song with a fine rhythm.

Bonus Tracks from the 1999 reissue on Konk/Velvel (63467-79732-2)
'Good Day' (Extended edit) (Davies)
At almost a minute longer than the album track, this version was released on the 12" single in Britain.

'Summer's Gone' (Extended edit) (Davies)
Again, almost a minute longer than the album track and released on the 12" single in Britain.

Think Visual (1986)

Personnel:
Ray Davies: vocals, rhythm guitar, keyboards, harmonica
Dave Davies: lead guitar, vocals, keyboards
Jim Rodford: bass, backing vocals
Bob Henrit: drums, percussion
Ian Gibbons: keyboards, backing vocals
Additional personnel:
Mick Avory: drums ('Rock 'N' Roll Cities')
Kim Goody: backing vocals ('Think Visual')
Producer: Ray Davies
Running time: 44:22
Recorded at Konk Studios, London (January, June-August 1986)
Release date: 17 November 1986
Original UK label and catalogue number: London Records LONLP 27
Chart positions: UK: –, US: 81, Australia: 97

The *Return To Waterloo* soundtrack was released in America only, on 1 July 1985, in the middle of what would be the first of a couple of quiet years for the band. There were only a few live dates in the US during the first half of the year, and a few more in September, then everything fell quiet. The band had decided to leave Arista, and during the last three months of 1985, negotiations were taking place with other companies. They eventually signed with MCA in America and London Records in the UK.

1986 proved to be an even quieter year for the band, although it began with Ray marrying his third wife, Pat Crosbie. There was also the release of the Julien-Temple-directed film *Absolute Beginners*, which despite having such luminaries as Ray Davies and David Bowie in the cast, was a spectacular flop.

The only Kinks-related events for the year were the recording and release of their first album for MCA/London, but even *that* had its problems. Ray wanted it to be a concept album – an idea that probably rang alarm bells at the record company considering what happened sales-wise with previous concepts. They wanted the band to concentrate on touring and promoting the album, whereas Ray had the idea of taking the spiv character from 'Come Dancing', and having him as an older man running a video shop and illegally copying films in the back room. As video shops were opening at a vast rate at this time, it was a pretty contemporary idea.

The concept sees the light of day in the track 'The Video Shop'. A compromise was reached, and it must've led to Ray being a bit rushed, as the album is not generally regarded as a classic Kinks set. It's not bad, in most people's eyes, but it could've been better.

The cover design and photography were by Richard Evans and Andrew Ellis – predominantly black with the band name (a red 'The' and white 'Kinks') and the album title (a white 'Think' and grey 'Visual'). Between the s and u of 'Visual', we have a picture of a female bodybuilder sitting in a typical pose. On the reverse, the 'Think' is grey and 'Visual' white, and instead of an 'I' in 'Think', we have the tracklist and a photo of Ray with a knowing look on his face as if he's asking us to think.

When the album was released in November, it was possibly caught in the Christmas rush and overshadowed by the plethora of compilation albums that seem to come out in the lead-up to the festive season. Also, the law of diminishing returns seems to have kicked in because of the slightly lower quality of the songs. Either way, it was a poor seller, reaching its highest chart position – 81 – in America in January 1987 (their worst chart peak since *Preservation Act 2* in 1974). It barely crept into the top 100 in Australia, sidling up to 97. And of course, you can forget Britain. However, of the two singles released in The Kinks' homeland, the first – 'How Are You' – was a chart entry, reaching 86. It fared better in America, climbing to 16. The UK's second single, 'Lost And Found', didn't chart there, and only reached 37 in America. There had been a single released in America before either of the aforementioned singles – 'Rock 'N' Roll Cities' was released in November 1986. It didn't chart but was a radio hit reaching 37 on the Mainstream Rock Tracks chart.

'Working At The Factory' (Davies)

This is about blue-collar life on an assembly line. The singer was programmed at school to be working in a factory. 'Then music came and gave new life to me'. But then he realises that a life in music is just like being in another kind of factory – probably hinting at the way Ray was supposed to be a hit machine in the 1960s. He even gets a cheeky line in alluding to those times, singing 'Never wanted to be like everybody else'. This mid-tempo rock song was the B-side to 'How Are You' in America.

'Lost And Found' (Davies)

UK release: London Records, LON 132, 3 April 1987. Producer: Ray Davies. Chart positions: Did not chart

'Lost And Found' was inspired by Hurricane Gloria – the grade-four storm which raged along the North-Eastern coast of the USA from 16 September to 4 October 1985. It describes a New York couple who lost each other just before the storm was due to hit but found each other just in time. Ray also sticks in a comment that man can never beat nature: 'This thing is bigger than the both of us/It's gonna put us in our place'.

It was released as a single in the US. There was a video made featuring an orchestra and the band members. It's a quieter song with a more emotive vocal. As with most of the album's songs, there's heavy use of keyboards (at one point simulating a steel band). Perhaps Ray wanted a more orchestral feel (hence the orchestra in the video) without using an actual orchestra. There's also a great and thoughtful guitar solo from Dave.

Strangely, 'Killing Time' was the flip side, as it had been on the previous single. This single didn't chart, but as with 'Rock 'N' Roll Cities', it reached 37 on the Mainstream Rock Tracks chart, making it a moderate radio hit.

'Repetition' (Davies)

It's always a source of wonder that Ray Davies could put himself in the mind of the ordinary man – a title that could never be attributed to Ray himself. He'd been living the live of a pop star for over 20 years now but still managed to write a chillingly-accurate tale of someone whose days are all the same: 'Every single day is just a repetition/It's always been that way'. Ray seems to have a penchant for writing up-tempo, happy sounding songs with depressing lyrical content, and this was one of them. He does like messing with our minds.

On a personal note, I feel that the guitar riff in the chorus has its origins in the intro to 'Everybody's A Star (Starmaker)' from *Soap Opera*.

'Welcome To Sleazy Town' (Davies)

The B-side to 'Rock 'N' Roll Cities' in the US. Ray is returning to the theme that inspired his *Preservation* albums. The big corporations buy up vast parts of the city, and where the people used to hang out is now a shopping mall and car parks.

This is a bluesy-sounding song: a style that Ray hadn't done for a while.

'The Video Shop' (Davies)

When the factory in which he worked closed down, this song's protagonist (We think it could be the spiv from 'Come Dancing', and the intro seems to have similarities to that track) takes out a bank loan and opens a video shop – people can now get away from their lives and enter the world presented to them on videotapes. But he is being a bit naughty:

I've got a bootleg version of *Citizen Kane*
A secondhand copy of *Psycho*
I've taped them off the telly
So you shouldn't complain

Ray goes in for a bit of reggae on this one. Is the video shop in Notting Hill, perhaps?

'Rock 'N' Roll Cities' (Dave Davies)

US single A-side. This song is a prime example of The Kinks' perversity. For years, Dave Davies and Mick Avory were getting on each other's nerves and just didn't get on. So, what happens on the first full album since Mick's departure? He plays on what is one of Dave's best rock songs in years. And what's more, Dave actually praised him: 'I really liked Mick's drumming on 'Rock 'N' Roll

Cities''. For this blistering 1980s rock anthem, I think Dave had been listening to Kiss, as the song's no-nonsense power is similar to their style.

The video to promote the track has a story of Ray going missing, and the rest of the band tries to find either him or a replacement. In the end, he is found. Dave's wife in the video was played by Marina Sirtis, who played Deanna Troi in the TV series *Star Trek: The Next Generation*. Dave sings lead, as he does on nearly all his songs. It didn't chart but reached 37 on the Mainstream Rock Track chart.

'How Are You?' (Davies)
UK release: London Records, LON 119, 22 December 1986. Producer: Ray Davies. Chart positions: UK: 86, US: 16, Australia: –

The original 'How Are You' demo recorded in January 1986 was so good, in Ray's opinion, that he used the demo vocal on the finished track. It's about how the singer is reminiscing with an old friend, but later on, the meeting turns sour, as he says 'I bet you're making all the same mistakes', but then says 'No offence'. A video was made featuring Ray to promote this mid-tempo pop song. The video shows Ray walking his dog and thinking about the time before his partner left him. We also see footage of The Kinks in the studio, but Dave is missing from the line-up. The single was a decent US hit, climbing into the top 20, and amazingly also entered the British chart: albeit at a lowly 86.

'Think Visual' (Davies)
The album's title track is an attack on video culture – an example of Ray biting the hand that feeds him. In the 1980s, a record had little chance of being a success if it didn't have an eye-catching video to go with it. Ray must've considered them a necessary evil (and a way to satisfy his acting urges). This song kicks along at a fair pace (mirroring the fast pace of the world in which the song is set), with jangly guitars very much in evidence throughout.

'Natural Gift' (Davies)
Ray sees a girl walking down the street, and she obviously has a natural gift to make people sit up and take notice of her: 'She looks like a prima donna'. He then tells us that it's within ourselves to find our own natural gifts. Another fast one here, and very 1980s in feel (Check out the Frankie Goes To Hollywood synthesizer blasts, similar in sound to their 'Two Tribes'), but we do get a typical Dave guitar riff from time to time and some funky bass from Mr. Rodford.

'Killing Time' (Davies)
B-side to both 'Lost And Found' and 'How Are You' in the UK.

'Killing Time' is about ennui. We are all waiting around and killing time until something happens. There is always something about to make your life better:

'Still I can smile at what I find/Waiting 'round and killing time'. Ray slows the pace a bit after the exertions of the album's previous two numbers.

'When You Were A Child' (Dave Davies)

Dave sings lead on his second song on the album. Ray must've been giving him more say in the records to keep him happy – this was the second album in a row where Dave had two songs. With lines like 'What was it like when you were a child?/Did you see the world in a different light?', Dave appears to be looking back on his childhood and how his feelings have changed as he has matured. His crunching guitar underlines this song, which ends the album at a fast tempo. As with his other offering on *Think Visual*, Dave's singing voice (at least on the verses) has reduced in pitch.

As mentioned earlier, most people seem to think that this album is pretty weak when you measure it against the rest of The Kinks canon, but the album has many highlights and is very underrated.

The Road (1988)

Personnel:
Ray Davies: lead vocals, guitar
Dave Davies: lead guitar, lead and backing vocals
Jim Rodford: bass, backing vocals
Bob Henrit: drums
Ian Gibbons: keyboards, backing vocals
Producer: Raymond Douglas Davies
Running time: 54:23
Recorded at Merriweather Post Pavilion, Columbia (29 June 1987); Mann Music
Center, Philadelphia (1 July 1987); Konk Studios, London (September 1987)
Release dates: UK: 23 May 1988, US: 11 January 1988
Original UK label and catalogue number: London Records LONLP 49
Chart positions: UK: –, US: 110
Tracklisting: 'The Road' (Davies), 'Destroyer' (Davies), 'Apeman' (Davies), 'Come
Dancing' (Davies), 'Art Lover' (Davies), 'Cliches Of The World (B Movie)' (Davies),
'Think Visual' (Davies), 'Living On A Thin Line' (Dave Davies), 'Lost And Found'
(Davies), 'It (I Want It)' (Davies), 'Around The Dial' (Davies), 'Give The People
What They Want' (Davies)

Towards the end of the 1980s, things quietened down a bit. Both Dave and Ray
had a few problems. Firstly, their mother died, and then Ray was admitted to
hospital for what they thought would be a heart bypass operation. However,
they found that his problem was, in fact, a blood clot, which the doctors dealt
with. Understandably, the band was generally inactive at the start of 1988 but
released the live album *The Road* – initially in America in January and in May in
Britain. To promote it, the band performed a handful of late-spring dates in the
US, and a short British tour followed soon after.

Some shows had been recorded in 1987, and the tracks on *The Road* came
from two of those concerts. Recorded a couple of days apart in Columbia and
Philadelphia, the tracks were generally regarded as 'workmanlike' rather than
anything special. But it is a good representation of a Kinks show as both Ray and
Dave entered their 40s (When the album was recorded, Dave had just turned
40, and Ray had his 43rd birthday just eight days before the Columbia show). It
transpires that the album's songs were all recorded at the Philadelphia gig, with a
section of 'Lost And Found' from the Columbia gig, spliced in.

The front cover has a stylised picture of an American desert road
disappearing into the distance (It could even be the one where Forrest Gump
ended his marathon run in the film), with the name of the band at the top.
There's a yellow road sign with the band name and album title, and the word
'Live' writ large. The back cover has another – this time winding – road with a
car heading away, and a track listing.

Unusually, there are two tracks on this live album that hadn't been heard
before: the title track and 'It (I Want It)'. 'The Road' had been recorded

especially for the album in Konk Studios in September 1987, and 'It (I Want It)' was a live track recorded at the Philadelphia gig.

Sadly, the album didn't receive the best reviews, and it managed to scrape up to only 110 in the American charts. The songs were all fairly recent, with the oldest one being 'Apeman'. Dave's 'Living On a Thin Line' from the *Word Of Mouth* album was his sole composition here. People have stated that the album's musicianship is 'workmanlike', meaning it as a criticism. But the album is a far cry from being bad – the musicianship, as ever, is excellent.

Just one single was taken from the album: 'The Road' b/w 'Art Lover'. It was released on the same day as the album in America (where it climbed to a creditable 14 in the charts), and a week before the album release in the UK (where it did nothing).

Single Release:
'The Road' (Davies) b/ w 'Art Lover' (Davies)
UK release: London Records, LON 165, 16 May 1988, US: 11 January 1988. Producer: Ray Davies. Chart positions: UK: –, US: 14, Australia: –

This was recorded in the studio but has crowd noises added at the end. Ray is citing some observations about life on the road – some good and some bad. This is a very good song and deserved to do better in the charts, although it reached a very decent 14 in America.

This live version of 'Art Lover' (from the *Give The People What They Want* album) is full of delicate guitar-playing, as Ray slows down a bit. In a nod to the American audience, he replaces the word 'Spangles' with 'candy', as not many Americans would've heard of the popular British confection.

UK Jive (1989)

Personnel:
Ray Davies: vocals, guitar, keyboards
Dave Davies: lead guitar, vocals
Jim Rodford: bass, backing vocals
Bob Henrit: drums, percussion
Ian Gibbons: keyboards, backing vocals
Additional personnel:
Mark Haley: additional keyboards ('Down All The Days (Till 1992)')
Mick Avory: drums, percussion ('Entertainment')
Producers: Ray Davies; Dave Davies ('Bright Lights', 'Perfect Strangers')
Running time: 51:37
Recorded at Konk Studios, London (June 1981, December 1988 to April 1989)
Release date: 2 October 1989
Original UK label and catalogue number: London Records 828 165-1
Chart positions: UK: –, US: 122

The 1980s were drawing to a close, and the momentum The Kinks had built up during the decade's first four years had diminished considerably. The band was touring less, and the time between studio releases was increasing. *UK Jive* was released a full three years after *Think Visual*, and as this was the longest gap between studio albums since the band started, many thought the band had had its day. Not so, as Ray Davies had been putting together some hard-hitting songs. He was now writing the songs he wanted to write, and was not looking for hit singles. Unfortunately, the fickle record-buying public was still thinking in terms of The Kinks as a singles' band, and if indeed they wanted anything from The Kinks, they wanted another hit like 'Waterloo Sunset' or 'You Really Got Me'. The band members of course were older now and trends had changed. After all, if Status Quo couldn't get played on BBC Radio One, what chance had The Kinks?

This album was not without its problems – it wouldn't be a Kinks record if something hadn't happened. Dave Davies wrote three songs for the album – more than on any previous record – but then Ray took a decision to remove two of them, leaving it as a ten-track album. Dave had had enough of his brother's machinations, and actually left the band (again). This split didn't last long, and he was back in time for a short tour in September 1989 to promote the release. Ray explained to Dave that he'd cut the tracks for the good of the album, but Dave (as he wrote in his autobiography) reckoned that it was rivalry and that Ray didn't want him having too much album input. The two tracks in question *did* see the light of day, as they were tacked onto the end of the cassette release and the CD.

There was another change of personnel, as Ian Gibbons left the band at the end of the recording sessions, and Mark Haley was brought in as a replacement, playing on one track. I doubt this was acrimonious, as Ian rejoined the band in 1993 and also accompanied Ray Davies on his solo outings.

Mark Haley is a Portsmouth-born musician with vast experience. He had appeared in the charts in 1981 as part of the 'Stars On 45' single. Since his tenure in The Kinks, he's been part of the Monkees' touring band and The Rubettes. As of September 2021, he was a member of The Equals.

Mick Avory also appears on the album. The track 'Entertainment' was recorded in June 1981 when he was still an active member of The Kinks.

The album cover featured photography by Trevor Rogers, and the front cover showed a black jacket and white shirt on a hanger (with a Union Jack handkerchief in the top pocket). The arms are akimbo (maybe suggesting a shrug). The band name and album title separate this from a pair of boots. The back has a track listing, a photo of a burning Union Jack, and four black-and-white blocks depicting a house, a dancing couple, the Union Jack and the stars of the European community flag. And since some of the songs are about Britain and its relationship with Europe and the world, we are getting a hint as to the contents of the album.

Sadly, *UK Jive* continued the downward trend of The Kinks' fortunes, as it only charted in the US, and then at a lowly 122. Perhaps the poor showing in America was due to the Britishness of the songs. It's a shame, really, as there are some good songs on here, and the sound is as polished as The Kinks would ever get, with all musicians performing at their best.

Two singles were lifted from the album: 'Down All The Days (Till 1992)' and 'How Do I Get Close'. Neither charted in Britain, but both managed some sort of success in America, with the former reaching 81. The latter didn't chart as such but reached 21 on the Mainstream Rock Tracks chart.

'Aggravation' (Davies)

A slow start before launching into a full-on rocker. Ray is railing against the aggravation of modern life, such as traffic jams and the fact that even though we won the war, the roads are full of German and Japanese cars, and he's close to cracking and being violent. It's Ray at his xenophobic best lyrically.

'How Do I Get Close' (Davies)

UK release: London Records, LON 250, 4 October 1989. Producer: Ray Davies. Chart positions: UK: –, US: 21

On this song, the singer wants to be close to someone, but everything is superficial and we're 'Living in a world where flesh is cheap'. It's slower than most of the *UK Jive* album and is very 1980s AOR – almost like a follow-up to 'A Little Bit Of Emotion' from the *Low Budget* album. It was the second single from *UK Jive* and reached 21 on the American Mainstream Rock Tracks chart. In Britain, the B-side of the single was 'Down All The Days (Till 1992)', and in America, 'War Is Over'.

'UK Jive' (Davies)

A rock and roll pastiche with a great jive rhythm. But things aren't always what they seem, as even though we've had a great time in the pub on a Saturday night, mum is annoyed that dad has spent all his wages and has 'forgot the inflation'. The lyrics state 'swing to the left, then back to the right' and 'swing both ways'. Is Ray talking politics or slyly introducing the concept of bisexuality?

'Now And Then' (Davies)

This is one of Ray's nostalgia pieces and is a slow number with plaintive lyrics about how 'mighty corporations and politicians rule the land'. He bemoans the fact that 'It's too bad the simple ways came sadly to an end'.

'What Are We Doing?' (Davies)

Ray is having doubts about the world in this up-tempo number, with what sounds a bit like the horn section from Earth Wind and Fire. He's wondering what he's doing in a world like this. He even gets in a dig about pollution, with the lines 'Why are we standing in the acid rain/Watching industrial waste trickling down the drain?'. Ray shows some more of his genius – as with quite a few of his songs – by disguising dark subject matter with a happy-sounding melody.

'Entertainment' (Davies)

Recorded in 1981 with Mick Avory on the drums, this rock number seems to foretell the future, with the population seemingly craving more and more sensationalism. He could see where things were heading, saying that all they want is 'sex violence, murder and rape'. Ray must have had a crystal ball.

'War Is Over' (Davies)

B-side to 'How Do I Get Close' in the US. This is apparently a commentary on the fact that there are old soldiers still around who won the war to make the world a better place, but we have forgotten them now, and more importantly, we seem to have forgotten what it is they were fighting for — another dark song with an upbeat melody.

'Down All The Days (Till 1992)' (Davies)

UK release: London Records, LON 239, 25 September 1989, 2 October 1989 (US)
Producer: Ray Davies b/w 'You Really Got Me' (Live) (Davies). Chart positions: UK: –, US: 81, Australia: 97
'Down All the Days (Till 1992)' was the album's first single in the UK (and strangely, the B-side to the second). It's a guardedly-optimistic song about European harmony, with some snippets of French, German and Italian. It's

a great mid-tempo rock song and reached 81 in America and scraped into the top 100 in Australia, peaking at 97. Of course, it didn't chart in Britain. The significance of 1992 was the Treaty of Maastricht, which was meant to significantly strengthen the European Union. There are even some celebratory church bells.

The single's B-side is a rendition of 'You Really Got Me' recorded on 1 July 1987 at the Mann Music Center, Philadelphia. It was probably left off the live *The Road* album as Ray wanted that particular album to showcase the more recent Kinks material.

'Loony Balloon' (Davies)

Despite the upbeat tone, this is like the majority of album: pretty dark. Basically, the world's gone mad. The highlight of this track for me is the 'military' snare drum from Bob Henrit, as it's something you don't expect from The Kinks., My overall impression is that the track has a 'sing-song' quality.

'Dear Margaret' (Dave Davies)

Dave's tirade against British Prime Minister Margaret Thatcher. 'Dear Margaret, I trusted you', he sings, 'Don't you let me down'. The protagonist is showing their political leanings, but now may be rethinking the wisdom of his vote. As with many of Dave's compositions, it's a rock number bordering on blues with crunching guitar (a bit like a slightly slower ZZ Top).

Bonus Tracks on cassette and CD
'Bright Lights' (Dave Davies)

Written and produced by Dave, this was one of the songs Ray cut from the original album. Dave seems to be singing about the breakup of a relationship, and he looks back to when the protagonist and the girl in question first met at a New York fashion show. The bright lights are the lights of the show and, indeed, the city. A typical Dave Davies rocker.

'Perfect Strangers' (Dave Davies)

This was the second Dave track (produced by Dave) that Ray cut from the album. The lyrics seem to suggest that the singer sees a person who is a stranger, but he sees 'something in your eyes', and they have a connection. Dave's strident vocal dominates the song, which has a great rock rhythm with a thudding bass drum and strong snare. The opening guitar riff is rather reminiscent of Deep Purple's 'Smoke On The Water'.

Phobia (1993)

Personnel:
Ray Davies: lead and backing vocals, rhythm guitar, keyboards
Dave Davies: lead guitar, lead and backing vocals
Jim Rodford: bass, backing vocals
Bob Henrit: drums
Producer: Raymond Douglas Davies
Running time: 76:10
Recorded at Konk Studios, London (September 1990 to February 1992)
Release date: 29 March 1993
Original UK label and catalogue number: Sony/Columbia Records 472 489-2
Chart positions: UK: –, US: 166

As the world entered the 1990s, The Kinks began to take more of a back seat in the music world, but yet the decade started on a high. On 17 January 1990, The Kinks were inducted into the Rock and Roll Hall of Fame at the fifth annual gala at the Waldorf Astoria Hotel in New York. Present for the awards were Ray, Dave, Mick Avory and original bassist Pete Quaife, who had travelled across the border from his new home in Canada, where he was working as an airbrush artist.

The plaudits didn't end there. On 2 April, Ray and The Kinks were given an award for Special Contribution To British Music at the 35th Ivor Novello Awards at London's Grosvenor House Hotel. This particular award was timely, as Britain was now in the throes of Britpop, with bands like Oasis and Blur citing The Kinks as an influence.

1991 saw the band gain a new manager in Nigel Thomas, and he helped broker a deal with Columbia Records for a new album, and a five-track EP was released in December. Recording sessions for the new album began in September 1990. But as with the majority of albums, there were problems. Initially, the two brothers worked well together, and Dave recalls that the first song they worked on was titled 'Close To The Wire'. He also contributed 'It's Alright (Don't Think About It)', and some sources state that 'Drift Away' was a Ray and Dave co-write.

Dave was also frustrated that the album was taking too long to record, with some songs taking three months to write, and Ray kept saying the songs weren't quite right. Then, just before the album was released, new manager Nigel Thomas passed away. Ray took over some of the managerial duties and kept the project on schedule.

Phobia was eventually released on 29 March 1993, over a year after the recording sessions were completed, and the first thing that people noticed was that the band was back to being a quartet (Ray, Dave, Jim Rodford and Bob Henrit), with Ray dispensing with a keyboard player and handling the keyboards himself (though Mark Haley was still part of the touring band). Also, this was the first Kinks album to be released primarily as a CD, and therefore, the running time was a shade over 76 minutes, with 17 tracks if you count the

38-second track 'Opening', and 'Did Ya', which is classed as a bonus track. This is also the only Kinks studio album to not feature Mick Avory on any track.

The cover was a departure from the norm, as befitting the CD format, and was a fold-out sheet with the lyrics and credits included. The front cover was a picture of Ray and Dave looking as though they were trying to hide from the camera, along with the band name and title. Also apparent is part of a painting showing burning buildings and animals hanging from trees. When folded out, this illustration is continued, showing people panicking in the streets, watched by a hissing cat and a pigeon. The back cover has a red background, a tracklisting and a picture of two children: a toddler and a baby, who are probably meant to represent Ray and Dave. The illustration was by British artist Sue Coe, who was living in America at the time and often depicted social commentary and animals in her works. She was brought up near a slaughterhouse in Staffordshire, and she often comments on animal cruelty. Photography was by Wigan-born Kate Garner, who'd been a member of the pop group Haysi Fantayzee. The whole thing was directed by Nicky Lindeman and Christopher Austopchuk.

Phobia was released as the band were finishing a UK tour, and they immediately set off for a short US tour which heralded more live dates. Prestigious British shows at the Glastonbury Festival on 27 June and the Royal Albert Hall on 11 July preceded a full arena tour in America, which ended at the beginning of September.

Sadly, the touring didn't help the sales of the album, which only charted for one week in the US, reaching 166, 92 in Germany, and didn't chart at all in the UK. However, reviews were generally good, and Ray was particularly upbeat about it, being reported as saying he thought he'd made a good hit record.

The songs were diverse, covering many subjects – including social commentary and sibling rivalry – and was highly regarded by the band's fans. But unfortunately for the fans – and for music in general – *Phobia* was the last-released studio album The Kinks... so far.

'Opening' (Davies)
This is a fairly pointless 38 seconds of synthesizer and guitar, culminating in drums. This could serve as an intro to almost any song.

'Wall Of Fire' (Davies)
This guitar-dominated mid-tempo song has a heavy drum rhythm from Bob Henrit throughout, and is the first of two consecutive songs which feature social meltdown and catastrophe. Basically, this lyric is about keeping going when everything is falling apart. The cover illustration appears to be a depiction of this track.

'Drift Away' (Davies)
The wistful intro to this song doesn't last, as we eventually get the full rock treatment. It's about wanting to drift away and escape the world of chaos that

we live in – with financial disasters, moral decline and the effects of global warming.

'Still Searching' (Davies)
The musicianship on this reflective ballad is sublime, with superb harmonies and excellent guitar and bass from Dave Davies and Jim Rodford. The protagonist is a drifter travelling around searching for his dreams and trying to achieve some sort of security.

'Phobia' (Davies)
The title track is a hard-hitting rocker which wouldn't be out of place on an Alice Cooper album. The tempo changes are a nice touch. It's a pretty dark song about the fears we try to keep hidden. Ray also lists some things that we are most afraid of.

'Only A Dream' (Davies)
UK release: Columbia Records, 659 922 2, 15 November 1993. Producer: Ray Davies. Chart positions: UK: 79, US: –, Australia: –
Ray says he wrote this one on a plane while thinking that the *Phobia* album was a bit dark and needed some humanity. It's fairly slow, with Ray's voice at the front of the mix, which is suitable as this is one of his story songs. Also, I think the intro is very much like 'Days'. The singer falls in love with a female, young exec he sees in a lift. The girl smiles and speaks to him. But then he starts to think it might be a dream, and he returns the next day. He does see her again, but this time she's talking to another man and ignores him completely. The allegory of the lift lifting you up and bringing you down is very clever.

'Don't' (Ray Davies)
Another mid-tempo story song about a walk through New York. The singer notices a crowd of people looking up at a man on a skyscraper ledge, telling him not to look down – and while they're all watching the man, the singer speculates about what could've driven the man to the brink of suicide.

'Babies' (Davies)
This rocker is similar in sound to those the band recorded in the early 1980s. Ray puts himself into the mind of a baby who's about to be born and is apprehensive about what he will encounter on the outside of the womb.

'Over The Edge' (Davies)
A typical rock song with a straightforward rhythm and the occasional jaunty keyboard riff. The singer is talking about being a victim of society. But he's on the edge of madness, and what's keeping him on the right side of sanity is the fact that he saw his neighbour succumb to madness.

'Surviving' (Davies)
A very strong drum and guitar intro lead into the song, with drums and vocals to the fore. This lyric is a commentary on the fact that we are all surviving despite things going against us and smiling 'through clouds of despair'.

'It's Alright (Don't Think About It)' (Dave Davies)
This is the first of two Dave Davies compositions on the album and the only one on which he sings the lead vocal. It's about the relentlessness of working life, how employers want your mind and body, and how you have to have hope and carry on. This is a typical Dave Davies rock song with a pounding rhythm: emphasising the unceasing plod of certain jobs.

'The Informer' (Davies)
A thoughtful song about two old friends drinking in a bar, who are on opposite sides of the Irish problem, and one of them has informed on the other. The song itself is a ballad, with soft electric guitar and the bass and drum parts sound very like the 1978 track 'Misfits'.

'Hatred (A Duet)' (Davies)
'Hatred (A Duet)' is the longest and most interesting track on the whole album. It's a fast song that has Ray and Dave trading lines, though Ray has the most to say. It's about sibling rivalry, the animosity between the two brothers, and their mutual feelings, with lines like 'It's the only thing that keeps us together' and 'The only thing we have in common'. Who wouldn't have loved to be a fly on the wall when they recorded this one?

'Somebody Stole My Car' (Davies)
'Somebody Stole My Car' begins with a car alarm sounding, and the song settles into a rhythm that sounds like it comes from a TV cop show, as it has overtones of *Peter Gunn* theme. The singer is bemoaning the fact that the city's law and order seem to be breaking down: especially as his car has been stolen. Listen carefully, as there's a nod to The Beatles' 'Drive My Car', with a 'Beep Beep, Beep Beep, Yeah!'.

'Close To The Wire' (Dave Davies)
A bluesy song which is the second Dave Davies track on the album, with vocals by both him and Ray. The song has a simple yet important message in that it appears we are more in love with material goods and are neglecting our spiritual health: a topic very close to Dave.

'Scattered' (Davies)
UK release: Columbia Records, 658 992 2, 12 July 1993. Producer: Ray Davies. Chart positions: Did not chart

'Scattered' is a country song with an intro reminiscent of 'Lola'. Ray has said that this song took ten years to write and is dedicated to his mother Annie Florence Davies and family friend Carol Bryans, who both died of cancer. Lyrically, it's about the aftermath of a mother's death, and 'scattered' refers to the fact that a mother's children are scattered around after they leave home.

'Did Ya' (Bonus track) (Davies)

This was a bonus track on the UK, Japanese and European versions of the album. It was released as a single in the Netherlands, and in the UK, it was the lead track on a five-song EP that had been released in 1991. This is a mid-tempo nostalgia piece containing a descending chord sequence similar to 'Sunny Afternoon', and even part of its lyric with the 'In the summertime' refrain. Ray is reminiscing about the 1960s and comparing them to the present day and how things are not as good – as evidenced in the line 'Did ya think it would get this bad?'.

To The Bone (1994)

Personnel:
Ray Davies: vocals, acoustic guitar, keyboards
Dave Davies: lead guitar, vocals
Jim Rodford: bass, vocals
Bob Henrit: drums, percussion
Ian Gibbons: keyboards, vocals
Producer: Ray Davies
Running time: 1:41:27 (1996 US expanded edition)
Recorded at Konk Studios, London (April 1994) and at various live concerts (August 1993 to April 1994)
Release dates: UK: 3 October 1994, US: 15 October 1996
Original UK label and catalogue number: Konk Records KNKLP 1
Chart positions: Did not chart

Following the release of *Phobia*, The Kinks toured hard to promote it throughout 1994 and 1995, but the band – that is to say Ray and Dave – were drifting apart even more. In 1994, Ray released what was called an 'unofficial biography', titled *X Ray*. It's significant that Ray got his sisters to read it, and they all liked it, especially Gwen. And he insisted that Mick Avory read the parts that related to him. Apart from one or two minor amendments, he, too, was happy with it. Dave, however, was kept in the dark and didn't even know about the book until it was published. He did read it and was reported as saying that he enjoyed it.

Eighteen months later, Dave also published an autobiography titled *Kink*, and it was a very frank recounting of his life, warts and all. Ray wasn't exactly enamoured of Dave's book, and according to Dave, Ray rang the Konk offices and said, 'I think this is going to be the end of The Kinks'.

In October 1994, the band released *To The Bone* – a mixture of live recordings and songs recorded in a semi-acoustic format in front of a small audience on 11 April 1994 at Konk Studios. It was originally released as a single CD in the UK, but two years later was issued as a two-CD set in the US – with extra tracks but leaving out two tracks from the single CD ('Waterloo Sunset' and 'Autumn Almanac'). Ray decided to sequence the running order by interspersing the live tracks with those recorded at Konk, as he says in the liner notes to the US release: 'I make no excuses for the live concert tracks being cut in and out of the unplugged sessions. I think this gives the record an edge. It is also very characteristic of The Kinks. Just when you think you are comfortable and you slurp into your easy-listening mode, they snap back in live concert so that you have to sit up and take notice'.

There were two different album covers. The single-CD UK version was black with the band name and title in white, along with a colourised x-ray image of a skill. The US version was a sepia image of a guitar fret being grasped by two hands (Ray and Dave?), with the band name and title in white. The reverse shows the track listing. The design was by Studio Q International, with photography by Gary Powell, Robert Ellis, Paul Cox and the Konk Studios archive. Sadly, the album failed to chart in any territory.

Tracklisting: 'All Day And All Of The Night' (Davies), 'Apeman' (Davies), 'Tired Of Waiting For You' (Davies), 'See My Friends' (Davies), 'Death Of A Clown' (Davies, Dave Davies), 'Waterloo Sunset' (Davies), 'Muswell Hillbilly' (Davies), 'Better Things' (Davies), 'Don't Forget To Dance' (Davies), 'Autumn Almanac' (Davies), 'Sunny Afternoon' (Davies), 'Dedicated Follower Of Fashion' (Davies), 'You Really Got Me' (Davies)

In 1994, a two-CD version was released in the US on Guardian/Konk Records (373 032-2). All tracks were recorded in front of a small audience at Konk Studios on 11 April 1994, except where noted.

'Animal' (Davies)

During the mixing of the album, Ray thought it would be a good idea to include a couple of new songs – both of which were recorded at Konk Studios between March and April 1996. He explains in the liner notes. They had both been songs that went down well at his solo gigs (Yes, Ray had been doing solo live shows, which again pointed to the fact that The Kinks' life was coming to an end). 'Animal' is a mid-tempo track played in a straight four, which Ray explains could be about the way his two cats Rusty and Rita interacted with each other.

'To The Bone' (Davies)

The second new song was one of three Ray had written with the same title. He renamed the other two 'Dentist's Chair' and 'Dog People', and said they'd probably turn up on a subsequent record. 25 years on, we have yet to see their release.

'To The Bone' has a similar tempo to 'Animal' and is about a relationship breakup where the singer returns home to find his girlfriend gone, and all she's left him are a couple of records that she had given him. As the records play, he remembers their relationship.

Other Extended Plays Not Already Discussed

Kinksize Hits

UK release: Pye Records, NEP24203, 15 Jan 1965. Producer: Shel Talmy, Chart position: UK: 3

'You Really Got Me' (Davies), 'It's All Right' (Davies), 'All Day And All Of The Night' (Davies), 'I Gotta Move' (Davies)

EP release featuring the band's third and fourth singles (the first two hits) and their attendant B-sides.

Dedicated Kinks

UK release: Pye Records, NEP24258, 15 Jul 1965. Producer: Shel Talmy. Chart position: UK: 7

'Dedicated Follower Of Fashion' (Davies), 'Till The End Of The Day' (Davies), 'See My Friends' (Davies), 'Set Me Free' (Davies)

Kinks

UK release: Pye Records NEP24296, 19 Apr 1968. Producers: Shel Talmy, Ray Davies Chart position: Did not chart

'David Watts' (Davies), 'Two Sisters' (Davies), 'Lazy Old Sun' (Davies), 'Situation Vacant' (Davies)

Percy

UK release: Pye Records, 7NX 8001, 2 April 1971. Producer: Ray Davies Chart position: Did not chart

'God's Children' (Davies), 'The Way Love Used To Be' (Davies), 'Moments' (Davies), 'Dreams' (Davies)

Did Ya

UK release: Columbia Records, 7N 15611, 1991. Producer: Ray Davies. Chart position: Did not chart

'Did Ya' (Davies), 'Gotta Move' (live) (Davies), 'Days' (1991 rerecording) (Davies) This is a 1991 re-recording of the 1968 song.

'New World' (Davies)

Clanging bells and a German-spoken count-in introduce this piece of electropop, and Ray sings about all the Europeans moving to America.

'Look Through Any Doorway' (Dave Davies)

Written and sung by Dave. This guitar-led song suggests that you should open up your heart like a doorway to see the good things in people

Waterloo Sunset '94

UK release: Konk/Grapevine Records, KNKCD 2, 17 October 1994. Producer: Ray Davies. Chart position: Did not chart

'Waterloo Sunset' (Davies)

This version was recorded at the Konk Studio sessions. It was on the UK single-CD release of the *To The Bone* album but was omitted from the two-CD version.

'You Really Got Me' (Live) (Davies)

Taken from the *To The Bone* album.

'Elevator Man' (Davies)

'Elevator Man' and 'On The Outside' were unreleased demos recorded in 1976. This one has a disco rhythm, and, as the title suggests, the singer works as an elevator man and tells us about the people who travel up and down. His mantra is 'Everybody goes up and everybody comes down'. The song was recorded as a demo during the *Sleepwalker* recording sessions.

'On The Outside' (Davies)

Another demo from the *Sleepwalker* sessions, and released on the 1998 reissue of that album (See *Seventies Albums*).

Other Releases Of Note

The Kinks Are The Village Green Preservation Society – Deluxe Edition (2004)

Original UK label and catalogue number: BMG/Sanctuary Records (2704679)
Discs one and two contained the stereo and mono versions of all songs from the 12 and 15-track versions of the album, along with a few alternate mixes. Side three was labelled 'Rarities' and comprised some alternate versions and previously very rare songs. These are listed below.

'Village Green' (Davies)

The orchestral instrumental version of the track, on which we can fully appreciate the orchestral arrangement by David Whitaker. Ray's vocal can be heard through headphone leakage.

'Misty Water' (Davies)

This is a song that was only available on *The Great Lost Kinks Album*, which had a limited release in America in 1973 and contained tracks from an unreleased American LP titled *Four More Respected Gentlemen*. Though recorded in May 1968, it sounds a lot like earlier Kinks material. This song appears twice: in stereo and mono mixes.

'Berkeley Mews' (Davies)

A stereo mix of the track that later appeared as the B-side to 'Lola' in 1970. 'Berkeley Mews' was recorded during the sessions for *The Village Green Preservation Society* but was later shelved.

   The lyrics are about a man who thought he'd found someone of equal intelligence to himself in the street of the title, only to find he was mistaken. There's some great honky-tonk piano from Nicky Hopkins, and brass at the end.

'Easy Come, There You Went' (Davies)

A 2004 remix of a track recorded in March 1968. A very rare beast this: a Kinks instrumental. It's an up-tempo song, heavy with mellotron and keyboards.

'Polly' (Davies)

Stereo version of the B-side to 'Wonderboy'.

'Animal Farm' (Davies)

A slightly rough stereo version of the song, that was delivered to Reprise (The Kinks' US record company) for a revised version of the US-only album *Four More Respected Gentlemen*.

'Phenomenal Cat' (Davies)

A stereo instrumental version (actually take 10) of the song, which was spelt incorrectly on some album covers, i.e. 'Phenominal Cat' on the original 15-track version of the album released in both Britain and America.

'Johnny Thunder' (Davies)

A 2004 stereo remix.

'Did You See His Name?' (Davies)

A mono version of the song that was commissioned for the BBC TV show *At The Eleventh Hour*. A stereo version is featured on *The Kinks BBC Sessions 1967-1977*.

'Mick Avory's Underpants' (Davies, Dave Davies)

A groovy instrumental recorded in March 1968 with just guitar, bass and drums. Apparently Mick used to wear distinctive underwear, and they thought it would make a great title.

'Lavender Hill' (Davies)

Recorded in August 1967. According to author Doug Hinman in his book 'All Day And All Of The Night', this may have been considered as the follow-up to 'Waterloo Sunset' but was passed over in favour of 'Autumn Almanac'. It's another refugee from *The Great Lost Kinks Album*, possibly inspired by the film *The Lavender Hill Mob*, and it's Ray longing for the London of his past. By the way, Lavender Hill is a real place, in Battersea.

'Rosemary Rose' (Davies)

Ray is comparing a girl he knew in his childhood to how she looks now. This is a soft and gentle 'pastoral' piece with some superb harpsichord from (I suspect) an uncredited Nicky Hopkins. This track woud not have been out of place on the original album.

'Wonderboy' (Davies)

A stereo mix of the hit, which was originally available on a budget compilation.

'Spotty Grotty Anna' (Davies, Dave Davies)

The Anna in question is one of London's most notorious groupies, and this song – actually the band jamming in the studio – was named after her. It's quite a funky piece.

'Where Did My Spring Go? (Davies)

A satirical song written especially for the BBC show *Where Was Spring?*. Ray is singing about the ageing process and asking where all his faculties went. (See also *The Kinks At The BBC*).

'Groovy Movies' (Davies)

Probably recorded in early-1969, this track was written by Ray but sung by Dave. It's a beat track with a brass backing. The protagonist is tired of playing in a rock and roll band and wants to make 'groovy movies' as a director. Is Ray hinting at his own aspirations here? If so, he realised his dream in 1984 with the TV movie for Channel Four in the UK: *Return To Waterloo*.

'Creeping Jean' (Dave Davies)

This was the B-side to Dave's fourth solo single, 'Hold My Hand'. It has very strong guitar, a vocal that predated punk by a number of years, a superb bassline and a catchy chorus. There was a change of recording studio here, as it was recorded at London's Polydor Studios.

'King Kong' (Davies)

B-side to 'Plastic Man'.

'Do You Remember Walter?' (Davies), 'Animal Farm' (Ray Davies), 'Days' (Ray Davies)

Three songs were recorded for BBC sessions in 1969, 1968 and 1970. For details of these, see *The Kinks At The BBC* below.

The Kinks At The BBC (2012)

Original UK label and catalogue number: Universal Music, 279 721-8. Release date: 21 August 2012. Chart position: Did not chart

In instances where recordings were too complex to be reproduced accurately in a BBC session (which typically lasted about three hours), the BBC sometimes allowed artists to use their commercially-released recordings with some overdubs, in order to achieve a unique variation of a track for broadcast. This happened on a number of Kinks sessions, and they are indicated with a (*).

Thanks to the BBC's policy of wiping tapes, many TV and radio recordings have been lost. However, some of the missing recordings have survived as bootleg recordings, thanks to fans recording them straight off the radio. Obviously, the quality of these tracks isn't great, but they do fill in some gaps. Those tracks are indicated thus: (**)

Recorded at The Playhouse Theatre, London on 7 September 1964. These were broadcast on *Saturday Club* on the BBC Light Programme (later Radio Two) on 19 September 1964. The interview was by Brian Matthew:
'Interview: Meet The Kinks', 'Cadillac' (Diddley), 'Interview: Ray Talks About 'You Really Got Me'', 'You Really Got Me', 'Little Queenie' (Berry)

Again recorded at The Playhouse Theatre, this time on 7 October 1964. These were broadcast on *Top Gear* (no, not the motoring programme) on the Light

Programme on 19 November 1964. Again, Brian Matthew was the interviewer:
'I'm a Lover, Not A Fighter' (Miller) (Lead vocal by Dave Davies with Ray on lead guitar), 'Interview: The Shaggy Set', 'You Really Got Me', 'All Day And All Of The Night'

A change of recording venue, as these songs were recorded at Piccadilly Studio One, London, on 9 December 1964, and broadcast on 12 December 1964 on the Light Programme's *Saturday Club*. As usual, Brian Matthew was the interviewer. 'Louie Louie' and 'Stop Your Sobbing' only exist as a bootleg recordings.
'I'm A Lover, Not A Fighter' (Miller) (Lead vocals by Dave Davies with Ray on lead guitar), 'Interview: Ray Talks About The USA', 'I've Got That Feeling', 'All Day And All Of The Night', 'Louie Louie' (**) (Berry), 'Stop Your Sobbing' (**)

With Brian Matthew again asking the questions, these were recorded at the BBC Maida Vale Studios, London, on 20 April 1965, and broadcast on *Saturday Club* on the Light Programme on 24 April 1965. However, 'Tired Of Waiting For You' was only broadcast during the week of 28 May 1965 on the BBC Transcription Service of *Top Of The Pops:*
'You Shouldn't Be Sad', 'Interview: Ray Talks About Records', 'Tired Of Waiting For You', 'Everybody's Gonna Be Happy'

Just a note about the BBC's Transcription Service here. There was a syndicated radio version of the BBC TV show *Top Of The Pops.* This was syndicated around the world, and the BBC would supply the recordings made in their studios on a vinyl disc, with voice-overs added by the DJ. Only a few hundred (500 tops) were pressed of each disc, and once they were played on the radio station where they were sent, they were generally forgotten. Luckily, enough survived, and are a valuable source of unreleased recordings. Brian Matthew was the host of *Saturday Club,* but left in 1965. He continued to record the interviews for the Transcription Service.

One of the plus sides of the Transcription Service recordings was that artists sometimes performed songs that were not necessarily hits. Such was the case with this session recorded at the BBC's Aeolian Hall on 6 August 1965. The group performed 'This Strange Effect', which wasn't commercially released. However, it was a massive hit in the Netherlands for singer Dave Berry.
   These recordings were broadcast on a special holiday show on The Light Programme on 30 August 1965. Entitled *You Really Got ... The Kinks*, the show also featured The Yardbirds and Kenny Lynch. Usually, this show was the domain of The Beatles, but the fab four were unavailable that year.
'This Strange Effect', 'Interview: Ray Talks about 'See My Friends'', 'See My Friends', 'Hide And Seek', 'Milk Cow Blues' (**) (Estes)

The Playhouse Theatre was the venue for these recordings on 10 August 1965, and the session was broadcast on *Saturday Club* on 4 September 1965. The interviewer is again Brian Matthew.

'Milk Cow Blues' (Estes), 'Interview: Ray Talks About Songwriting', 'Never Met A Girl Like You Before', 'Wonder Where My Baby Is Tonight' (featuring Dave Davies on lead vocal)

Back to The Playhouse Theatre on 13 December 1965 for this session, which was broadcast on *Saturday Club* on 18 December 1965. This appears to be the last time Brian Matthew did the interview. And strangely, this would be The Kinks' last BBC session for eighteen months. Dave Davies was lead vocalist on 'I Am Free', and co-lead vocalist on 'Milk Cow Blues'.

'Interview: Meet Pete Quaife', 'Till The End Of The Day', 'A Well Respected Man', 'Where Have All the Good Times Gone?', 'Milk Cow Blues' (**) (Estes), 'I Am Free' (**) (Dave Davies)

In effect, this was a Dave Davies special, as it featured Dave on lead vocals on all three songs. 'Death Of A Clown' was released as a Dave Davies solo single on 7 July 1967, with his composition 'Love Me Till The Sun Shines' on the B-side. This session was recorded at The Playhouse Theatre on 4 August 1967. 'Death Of A Clown' was only broadcast on *Saturday Club* the day after. The whole session – with interview by David Symonds – was syndicated by the Transcription Service for broadcast in September. The session also featured Nicky Hopkins on keyboards, and Rasa Davies (Ray's wife) on backing vocals. This would be the last time The Kinks would appear on BBC's Light Programme, as, on 30 September, the BBC's Light Programme, Third Programme and Home Service would become BBC Radio Two, Three and Four respectively. From then on, what was considered pop music would generally be broadcast on 'Wonderful' Radio One.

'Love Me Till The Sun Shines' (Dave Davies), 'Interview: Meet Dave Davies', 'Death Of A Clown' (Davies, Dave Davies), 'Good Luck Charm' (Koerner)

Back to BBC's Maida Vale for a six-track session on 25 October 1967, aided by Nicky Hopkins on piano. All six tracks were broadcast on Radio One's *Top* Gear show on 29 October 1967. However, for the Transcription Service, the session was split. 'Sunny Afternoon', 'Autumn Almanac' and 'Harry Rag' went out at the beginning of December 1967, and 'Mr. Pleasant', 'Susannah's Still Alive' and 'David Watts' at the end of December. Dave Davies sang lead on 'Susannah's Still Alive'.

'Sunny Afternoon', 'Autumn Almanac' (*), 'Harry Rag', 'Mr. Pleasant', 'Susannah's Still Alive' (Dave Davies), 'David Watts'

There was a gap of eight months before The Kinks were required for another radio session. This one was recorded at the BBC's Piccadilly Studios on 1 July 1968, and broadcast on Radio One's *Top Gear* show on 7 July 1968. The band was joined again by Nicky Hopkins on piano and organ, and Rasa Davies on backing vocals.

'Waterloo Sunset', 'Interview: Ray Talks About Working', 'Days'

The Kinks were back in The Playhouse Theatre again just a week later on 9 July 1968, to record a session for Radio One's *Saturday Club*, broadcast on 13 July 1968. After a short chat with Ray talking about his brother's solo work, Dave sang lead vocals on 'Love Me Till The Sun Shines' and 'Susannah's Still Alive'.

'Interview: Ray Talks About Dave's Solo Records', 'Love Me Till The Sun Shines', 'Monica', 'Susannah's Still Alive' (**) (Dave Davies), 'Days' (**)

Back to the same venue (The Playhouse Theatre) on 26 November 1968 for another session for *Saturday Club*, broadcast four days later on 30 November 1968. As the *Village Green* album had just been released, this was the first time Ray was able to talk about it and showcase a couple of tracks.

'Interview: Ray Talks About 'Village Green', 'The Village Green Preservation Society', 'Animal Farm' (*)

In 1969, Ray wrote five songs for the satirical BBC series *Where Was Spring?* This Ned-Sherrin-produced show only lasted for 12 episodes and featured Eleanor Bron and John Fortune. The Kinks recorded 'Where Did My Spring Go?' at the BBC's Riverside Studios on 28 January 1969 for the show, which was broadcast on BBC Two on 3 February. They were back on 4 February 1969 to record 'When I Turn Off The Living Room Lights', for the show on 10 February 1969. Sadly, due to the BBC's misguided policy of wiping shows, only these two songs survive. The other three songs written and recorded were: 'We Are Two Of A Kind', 'Let's Take Off Our Clothes' and 'Darling I Respect You'. The band didn't appear on the show, and the songs were animated using illustrations by Manfred Mann bassist Klaus Voormann: who'd supplied the striking album cover for The Beatles' *Revolver.*

'Where Did My Spring Go?', 'When I Turn Off The Living Room Lights'

After nearly four years, The Kinks were back at the Aeolian Hall studio to record a session with Radio One DJ Peter Symonds for his show *Symonds On Sunday.* The session took place on 2 April 1969 and was broadcast on Radio One on 13 April 1969. Strangely, the BBC's Transcription Service didn't see fit to broadcast the session until May and June the following year.

'Plastic Man' (*), 'King Kong' (*), 'Do You Remember Walter?' (*), 'Interview: Ray Talks About Rumours'

As we approached the end of 1969, Dave Lee Travis had become one of the most popular presenters on BBC Radio One, and The Hairy Monster – as Travis was nicknamed – featured The Kinks on a number of occasions. Their first session for Travis took place at the Camden Theatre, London, on 18 December

1969, and was broadcast on *The Dave Lee Travis Show* on 28 December 1969. The songs were all from the recently released *Arthur* album.
'Victoria' (*), 'Mr. Churchill Says' (*), 'Arthur' (*)

The Aeolian Hall, Studio Two was the venue for the band's second session for *The Dave Lee Travis Show*, recorded on 18 May 1970 and broadcast on Radio One on 31 May 1970. Dave Davies sang lead vocals on 'Mindless Child Of Motherhood', and Nicky Hopkins played keyboards on 'Days'.
'Interview: Ray Talks With Keith Altham', 'Lola' (*), 'Mindless Child Of Motherhood' (Dave Davies), 'Days' (*)

The Dave Lee Travis Show broadcast a specially-recorded version of 'Apeman' on 13 December 1970 on BBC Radio One. It had been recorded with the rest of the *Lola Versus Powerman And The Moneygoround* album. It was delivered to the BBC on 4 November 1970 – just before its official release – but why there was such a delay in broadcasting it, is unclear.
'Apeman' (*)

Three tracks from *Muswell Hillbillies* and one from *Everybody's In Showbiz* were recorded at Studio T1 in Kensington House, London on 5 May 1972. They were broadcast on BBC Radio One's *John Peel Show* on 16 May 1972. With the brass section of John Beecham (trombone), Alan Holmes (tenor saxophone, clarinet) and Michael Rosen (trumpet) filling out the sound, this session showcased the forthcoming single 'Supersonic Rocket Ship' and the future sound of the band as it entered its theatrical phase.
'Acute Schizophrenia Paranoia Blues', 'Holiday', 'Skin And Bone', 'Supersonic Rocket Ship'

A one-off track recorded at Morgan Studios delivered to the BBC towards the end of February 1973 and broadcast on BBC Radio One's *Dave Lee Travis Show* on 5 March 1973. In my opinion, this was a strange track to broadcast, as 'Here Comes Yet Another Day' was off the *Everybody's In Showbiz* album, which had been released the previous September.
'Here Comes Yet Another Day' (*)

A previously unvisited venue, as The Kinks set up in Studio One at Langham Studios, London, on 6 June 1974, to record three tracks for Radio One's *John Peel Show*. It was broadcast on 11 July 1974. This session showcased the *Preservation* albums, with 'Demolition' being from the first album and 'Mirror Of Love' and 'Money Talks' from the second. In keeping with the theatrical style of the recordings, the band were joined by John Beecham (trombone), Alan Holmes (tenor saxophone), Laurie Brown (trumpet), and backing vocalists Pamela Travis and Maryann Price.
'Demolition', 'Mirror Of Love', 'Money Talks'

BBC Radio One started their *In Concert* series in 1970, and it was The Kinks' turn to appear in 1974. Introduced by Alan Black and recorded before an invited audience at The Hippodrome Theatre in Golders Green on 14 July 1974, it was broadcast on 27 July 1974. Interspersed with hits, the concert featured the *Preservation* albums, with six songs performed from the two albums. The band was augmented by a brass section comprising John Beecham (tuba), Alan Holmes (clarinet) and Laurie Brown (trumpet). Pamela Travis and Claire Hamill supplied backing vocals. By now, The Kinks had built their own recording studio Konk, and later, Claire Hamill was signed as a solo artist to the Konk record label.

'DJ Alan Black Introduces 'In Concert'', 'Victoria', 'Here Comes Yet Another Day', 'Mr. Wonderful' (Holofcener, Weiss, Bock), 'Money Talks', 'Dedicated Follower Of Fashion', 'Mirror Of Love', 'Celluloid Heroes', 'You Really Got Me/All Day And All Of The Night', 'DJ Alan Black Talks About 'Preservation Act 2'', 'Daylight', 'Here Comes Flash', 'Demolition', 'He's Evil', 'Lola', 'Outro', 'Skin And Bone/Dry Bones' (Davies/Trad.)

As regards television, for pop and chart music, the most influential BBC show was BBC One's *Top Of The* Pops, which began on 1 January 1964 and ended on 30 July 2006. But for rock and (arguably) more adult music, there was *The Old Grey Whistle Test*, which was broadcast on BBC Two from 21 September 1971 until 1 January 1988. Presented from 1972 to 1978 by 'Whispering' Bob Harris, it became a tradition for the show to have a Christmas concert. In 1977, the honour of this prestigious slot fell to The Kinks.

As with the *In Concert* shows, they were recorded in front of an invited audience.

With Bob Harris and Alan 'Fluff' Freeman sharing hosting duties, the show was recorded and broadcast live from The Rainbow Theatre, London on 24 December 1977. It went out simultaneously on *The Old Grey Whistle Test* on BBC Two, and as *Radio One Sight 'N' Sound: The Kinks' Christmas Concert* in stereo on Radio One. This version is the radio broadcast (the TV version comes later), and the band is augmented by John Beecham (trombone, tuba), Alan Holmes (saxophone, clarinet), Nick Newall (saxophone), Mike Cotton (trumpet), Ray Cooper (percussion) and backing vocalists Debi Doss and Kim Goody.

'Alan Freeman Introduction', 'Juke Box Music', 'Bob Harris Introduction', 'Sleepwalker', 'Life On The Road', 'A Well Respected Man', 'Death Of A Clown' (Davies, Dave Davies) (Lead vocal: Dave Davies), 'Sunny Afternoon', 'Waterloo Sunset', 'All Day And All Of The Night', 'Slum Kids', 'Celluloid Heroes', 'Get Back In The Line', 'The Hard Way', 'Lola', 'Alcohol', 'Skin And Bone/Dry Bones' (Davies/Trad.), 'Father Christmas', 'You Really Got Me'

We had to wait until 1994 before a Kinks session was broadcast on the BBC again. It was on *The Johnnie Walker Show* on 1 January 1994 that a live recording from The Maida Vale Studios was unleashed upon the Radio One airwaves. Three tracks from the band's album *Phobia* were performed with 'Till The End Of The Day'. Dave Davies was unavailable at the time (After all, it was New Years' Day), and the more-than-capable Jakko Jakszyk took Dave's place on electric guitar.

'Interview: Ray Talks To Johnnie Walker', 'Phobia', 'Interview: Ray Introduces 'Over The Edge'', 'Over The Edge', 'Wall Of Fire', 'Till The End Of The Day'

The final BBC radio recording was later that year. Recorded at The Maida Vale Studios on 7 October 1994 for Radio One's *The Emma Freud Show*, the band performed five of their biggest 1960s hits.

'All Day And All Of The Night', 'Waterloo Sunset', 'I'm Not Like Everybody Else', 'Till The End Of The Day', 'You Really Got Me'

Colour Me Pop was a spin-off from the BBC 2 programme *Late Night Line-Up*. It only ran for a couple of years, but many big acts appeared, including Fleetwood Mac, Small Faces, Manfred Mann and The Move. Only a very few of these shows survive, and, sadly, the appearance by The Kinks is one of them. The show was recorded at the BBC Television Centre on 22 July 1968 and broadcast on BBC Two on 28 July 1968. The recordings on this release are again among those that were recorded by fans off the TV and are of bootleg quality. Dave Davies provides lead vocals on 'Death Of A Clown' and 'Lincoln County'.

'Dedicated Follower Of Fashion/A Well Respected Man/Death Of A Clown' (**) (Davies, Dave Davies), 'Sunny Afternoon' (*) (**), 'Two Sisters' (*) (**), 'Sitting By The Riverside' (*) (**),'Lincol n County' (*) (**) (Dave Davies), 'Picture Book' (*) (**), 'Days' (*) (**)

The above tracks comprised the first five discs of a six-disc set. Disc six was a DVD of television appearances, and for completists, I have included them in this book.

The Beat Room

The Beat Room was a short-lived music programme that ran for 29 episodes on BBC Two from 6 July 1964 to 29 January 1965. Of those 29 episodes, only one survives, and luckily, it's the one that features The Kinks, along with Tom Jones, Julie Rogers, John Lee Hooker and The Syndicats (with future Yes guitarist Steve Howe). This was recorded at the BBC Television Centre on 1 October 1964, and was broadcast on 5 October 1964.

'You Really Got Me', 'Got Love If You Want It' (Moore)

A Whole Scene Going

Another short-lived show from 1966, only 24 episodes of BBC One's *A Whole Scene Going* were made. The Kinks appeared on two episodes, but only this

one survives (Apparently only four of the 24 survive). Recorded at the BBC Television Centre on 8 June 1966 and broadcast on the same day, Pete Quaife was absent, as he'd recently been injured in a car crash, which left him out of action until November. John Dalton deputised for him during this time.
'Sunny Afternoon'

Top Of The Pops (1)
Sadly, many of The Kinks' appearances on the BBC flagship music show *Top Of The Pops*, have been wiped. Videotape was expensive back then, and the BBC, in its infinite wisdom (?!), decided to wipe some of its shows to re-use the tape. The result was that giant swathes of material were lost. Some dedicated people have scoured archives of television stations around the world, trying to recover as much as possible, and some success has been had. For instance, over 100 seemingly-lost episodes of *Doctor Who* have been found in such diverse places as New Zealand and Nigeria. However, *Top Of The Pops* was seen as disposable, and very few lost clips have been unearthed.

They had finally seen sense by 1970, so the edition broadcast on 18 June 1970 lives on. The Kinks performed 'Lola' just days after its release. The clip itself had been recorded at the Television Centre on 20 May 1970: a couple of weeks before the single came out (pun not intended).
'Lola'

Top Of The Pops (2)
On 6 January 1971, the band recorded 'Apeman' at the Television Centre for *Top Of The Pops*, and it was broadcast the next day.
'Apeman'

Old Grey Whistle Test (1)
The band returned to the Television Centre on 4 January 1972 for a slot on BBC Two's *The Old Grey Whistle Test*. Ray and band performed 'Have A Cuppa Tea' from the recently released *Muswell Hillbillies* album, and it was broadcast that same night.
'Have A Cuppa Tea'

Top Of The Pops (3)
When The Kinks returned to the charts with 'Come Dancing', a visit to *Top Of The Pops* was arranged. So, it was back to the Television Centre for a recording session on 24 August 1983, which was broadcast on the same day.
'Come Dancing'

The Late Show
After *The Old Grey Whistle Test* was cancelled, the BBC occasionally showed music performances on *The Late Show* – a magazine programme that went out

on BBC Two after *Newsnight*. The Kinks performed the single from *Phobia* on 25 March 1993 (prior to its July release) at the Television Centre, and it was broadcast later that night.
'Scattered'

Later With Jools Holland
The band recorded two more tracks from *Phobia* at the Television Centre on 25 March 1993 for the BBC Two show *Later With Jools Holland*. It was broadcast on the same day, along with a performance of 'Till The End Of The Day'.
'Over The Edge', 'Informer', 'Till The End Of The Day'

Top Of The Pops (4)
The Kinks' final appearance on *Top Of The Pops* was recorded and broadcast on 29 September 1994. The Television Centre was treated to a rousing version of the band's first hit – celebrating the fact that it was 30 years since it had topped the charts.
'You Really Got Me'

The Kinks At The Rainbow
The Kinks At The Rainbow packed a lot into its 45 minutes. It was broadcast on BBC One during the evening of 21 July 1972. This was a Friday evening, and news was just breaking of a series of at least 20 bombs exploding in Northern Ireland. The show went out after the six o'clock news, at 6:30. The programme featured concert footage filmed at The Rainbow Theatre, London, on 31 January 1972, interspersed with rehearsals and interviews recorded in January at The Archway Tavern in Highgate and Birmingham. The concert featured The Kinks with The Mike Cotton Sound (Mike Cotton: trumpet, John Beecham: trombone, tuba, Alan Holmes: saxophone, clarinet). This was one of the very few occasions when we heard some of the music that Ray had written for the film *The Virgin Soldiers*. 'Top Of The Pops' was illustrated by a conceptual film by Tom Taylor, and 'The Moneygoround' featured a live vocal over a backing track.
'Till The End Of The Day', 'Waterloo Sunset', 'Top Of The Pops', 'The Money-Go-Round', 'Sunny Afternoon', 'Virgin Soldiers', 'She Bought A Hat Like Princess Marina', 'Alcohol', 'Acute Schizophrenia Paranoia Blues', 'You Really Got Me' start here

In Concert
This *In Concert* appearance was recorded in front of an invited audience at the BBC Television Centre on 24 January 1973, and broadcast on BBC Two at 22.45 to 23.15 on 15 March 1973. The Mike Cotton Sound – with the same lineup as *The Kinks At The Rainbow* – accompanied the band, and for the last

two numbers, they were joined by a brass band and chorus conducted by Pip Williams.

'Victoria', 'Acute Schizophrenia Paranoia Blues', 'Dedicated Follower Of Fashion', 'Lola', 'Holiday', 'Good Golly Miss Molly' (Marascalco, Blackwell), 'You Really Got Me', 'Waterloo Sunset', 'The Village Green Preservation Society'

The Old Grey Whistle Test (3)

28 March 1977 saw the band back at the Television Centre, recording a show for *The Old Grey Whistle Test* which was broadcast on 26 April 1977. For this performance which showcased the *Sleepwalker* album, the band drafted in some extra personnel in the form of John Beecham, who played trombone and keyboards on 'Juke Box Music' and 'Full Moon' respectively; Nick Newall, who played saxophone on 'Juke Box Music' and extra keyboards on 'Full Moon'. Debi Doss and Shirlie Roden were the backing vocalists.

'All Day And All Of the Night', 'Sleepwalker', 'Life Goes On', 'Stormy Sky', 'Celluloid Heroes', 'Muswell Hillbillies', 'Full Moon', 'Life On The Road', 'Juke Box Music'

The Old Grey Whistle Test (4): The Kinks' Christmas Concert

This is the television broadcast of *The Kinks' Christmas Concert 1977*. All the details about this recording are covered in the section dealing with the radio broadcast. It was simultaneously broadcast on BBC Two from 10.00 to 11.00 p.m. on Christmas Eve 1977.

'Juke Box Music', 'Sleepwalker', 'Life On The Road', 'A Well Respected Man', 'Death Of A Clown' (Davies, Dave Davies), 'Sunny Afternoon', 'Waterloo Sunset', 'All Day And All Of The Night', 'Slum Kids', 'Celluloid Heroes', 'Get Back In The Line', 'Schoolboys In Disgrace', 'Lola', 'Alcohol', 'Skin And Bone/Dry Bones' (Davies/ Trad.), 'Father Christmas, 'You Really Got Me'

Late Night Line-Up

A rare non-musical piece which was recorded and broadcast on 5 August 1968 on BBC Two's *Late Night Line-Up: The Alan Price Show.* Ray and Dave were interviewed by Alan Price.

'Interview With Ray & Dave'

The Songs Of Ray Davies: Waterloo Sunset (1997)

Original UK label and catalogue number: Essential Records ESS CD 592, Producer: Raymond Douglas Davies, Running time: 133:02, Release date: 29 September 1997, Chart positions: UK: 96, US: –, Australia: –

This was a two-CD collection. The first CD was titled *The Singles Collection* and comprised 25 tracks: 23 Kinks tracks and two singles credited to Dave Davies. The Kinks singles released on Pye Records – up to and including 'Apeman' – are featured, along with some EP tracks.

The second CD is titled *The Songs Of Ray Davies: Waterloo Sunset* and contains a number of tracks from The Kinks and solo Ray Davies. There are remixes of some Kinks numbers, a couple of live tracks, unreleased tracks, and a couple of songs from Ray's *Return To Waterloo* project. This could be considered a Ray Davies solo album, but since many are Kinks records in the first place – and The Kinks play on some of the tracks – I thought it best to include it.

'The Shirt' (Unreleased demo recording)
This song could be the basis of a film and was recorded at Konk Studios. It's about a man who buys a shirt at a thrift shop In New York. There's a stain on the shirt, which he ignores, but he's later arrested for murder, as the stain is the blood of a murder victim. The song itself has a smooth jazz vibe, and Ray says that if he'd taken the song further, he would've added horns.

'A Rock 'N' Roll Fantasy' (Live)
A live version of the *Misfits* track, recorded in the mid-1990s at an unknown venue.

'Mr. Pleasant'
Mono version of the 1967 track that was the B-side to 'Autumn Almanac' in the UK.

'Celluloid Heroes' (Live)
Originally included on the *One For The Road* album. Recorded live on 11 November 1979 at the Volkshaus, Zurich, Switzerland.

'Voices In The Dark' (Remix)
A 1997 stereo mix of a track recorded in April 1985 at Konk Studios for the *Return To Waterloo* film. It was meant to be used over the film's end credits, but in the end, it wasn't. The girl's voice on the song is Ray's daughter Louisa.

'Holiday Romance'
Stereo mix of the song recorded in September 1974 at Konk for the *Soap Opera* album.

'Art Lover' (Remix)
A stereo mix of an alternative take of the song, recorded at Konk in May and June 1981 for the *Give The People What They Want* album.

'Still Searching'
Recorded again at Konk in late-1990, this is an alernative mix of a song from the *Phobia* album.

'Return To Waterloo' (Demo recording/Remix)
This is a stereo mix of a demo recorded at Konk in 1985 for the *Return To Waterloo* project. The traveller in the film is reflecting on how his day is going to pan out.

'Afternoon Tea'
Stereo mix of the 1967 song from the *Something Else* album.

'The Million-Pound-Semi-Detached' (Demo)
A stereo mix of a song recorded in spring 1989 at Konk. Apart from this release, it was only available on the six-CD set *Picture Book* released in December 2008. It was written around the time of the property boom in 1988.

'My Diary' (Demo)
A stereo mix of a song recorded at Konk: date unknown. This is the only known release for this track. The singer looks at his diary, and it's full of run-of-the-mill appointments. As he says, the diary is full, but his life is empty.

'Drivin'
A Stereo mix of the 1969 song from the *Arthur* album.

'Waterloo Sunset' (Stereo mix)
Stereo mix of the 1967 hit.

'Scattered'
Stereo mix of the track from the *Phobia* album, recorded in 1990.

There were also two US-only compilations released after The Kinks' deal with Reprise wasn't renewed in the early-1970s. The first -*The Kink Kronikles* – was released in 1972 and is a double vinyl album containing tracks covering the period 1966-1970.

The second is of more interest, as it features many tracks that had not been issued in the UK. Covering the same period as *The Kink Kronikles*, most of the tracks have subsequently surfaced on deluxe and special reissues. The track listing is as follows:

'Til Death Us Do Part', 'There Is No Life Without Love', 'Lavender Hill', 'Groovy Movies', 'Rosemary Rose', 'Misty Water', 'Mr. Songbird', 'When I Turn Off The Living Room Light', 'The Way Love Used To Be', 'I'm Not Like Everybody Else', 'Plastic Man', 'This Man He Weeps Tonight', 'Pictures In The Sand', 'Where Did My Spring Go?'

Solo Recordings

Both Ray and Dave Davies have released solo albums, with Dave's in 1980
being the first.

Ray Davies Solo Albums

Return To Waterloo (1985), The Storyteller (1998), Other People's Lives (2006),
Working Man's Café (2007), The Kinks Choral Collection (2009) (with the
Crouch End Festival Chorus,
See My Friends (2010) (with guest musicians), Americana (2017). Our Country:
Americana Act II (2018)

Dave Davies Solo Albums

AFL1-3603 (1980), Glamour (1981), Chosen People (1983), Bug (2002),
Fractured Mindz (2007), I Will Be Me (2013), Rippin' Up Time (2014),Decade
(2018)

Kast Off Kinks

The murky world of tribute acts has thrown up a plethora of live bands
wanting to celebrate the music of their favourite artistes. Some of them are
good, some bad, and some excellent. But in the end, they're all musicians
emulating their heroes.

Naturally, The Kinks have something different. Unlike the vast majority
of tribute bands, the main Kinks tribute contains ex-members of the band.
The Kast Off Kinks started life in 1994, and was formed for an annual charity
concert for Leukemia research, put together by John Dalton. The singer and
guitarist Dave Clarke – who takes the parts of both Ray and Dave Davies –
explains how he's usually the only non-Kink in the band: 'I was in a band called
Shut Up Frank with Mick Avory, and we were playing some Kinks songs in the
set. Dave Rowberry (Animals), Noel Redding (Hendrix) and Jim Leverton were
all at various times in the band. I had been to John Dalton's 50th birthday party
and played with him and a few others, so had met some of the usual suspects
around The Kinks, had also done some recording at Konk with Shut Up Frank
and others. John Dalton ran an annual fundraising gig for Leukemia research
at the Broxbourne Civic, where he and a lot of friends used to play a variety of
sets – some covers of other bands and some of their own. He decided it might
be fun to do a Kinks set, and since I was playing with Mick, I was roped in for
the gig on 9 October 1994 with Mick, Nobby (John Dalton) and the Baptist
(John Gosling). I think we played for about half an hour under the name of the
Juicers and had done one local gig as a warm-up. As far as I recall, we did a few
other gigs and very soon became the Kast Off Kinks: Nobby's idea, I think. The
band didn't start to do a great deal of gigs until Ian (Gibbons) joined when it
really ramped up. The first time Ray joined us on stage was at the annual fan
club bash. I can't remember which year and didn't know if he was going to
join us on stage or not. He has come regularly for a number of years now and
even came to Holland with us to do a show for the Dutch fan club. Dave has
never been to one of our gigs and has never been at the fan club bash since we
started doing it'.

It's a well-known fact that every former member of The Kinks has appeared
with The Kast Off Kinks, except one – and that is Dave Davies, who has stated
that 'I am not a Kast Off Kink'.

Through The Kinks Official Fan Club, the band have released three CDs.
In November 2001, they released a five-track EP titled *The Archway EP*:
recorded at GCMP Studios in Hoddesdon. This was followed in February
2010 by the live album *Live At The Brook*, which was recorded at The Brook
in Southampton. The third was another studio recording, titled *Orses For
Kourses*, recorded at Roundel Studios in Kent. This was released in February
2013.

The Archway EP contained the following tracks:
'Victoria', 'Schooldays', 'Powerman', 'God's Children', 'Muswell Hillbillies'

Live At The Brook **had these tracks:**
'Where Have All The Good Times Gone', 'Victoria', 'I Gotta Move', 'Stop Your
Sobbing', 'Days', 'Dead End Street', 'Till The End Of The Day', 'The Village
Green Preservation Society', 'Set Me Free', 'Apeman', 'Tired Of Waiting For You',
'Dedicated Follower Of Fashion', 'Better Things', 'All Day And All Of The Night'

Orses For Kourses **contained:**
'Muswell Hillbillies', 'Waterloo Sunset', 'Come Dancing', 'Set Me Free', 'Lola',
'Celluloid Heroes', 'A Well Respected Man', 'Sunny Afternoon', 'See My Friends'
'Autumn Almanac', 'You Really Got Me'

Afterword

At the time of this writing, *To The Bone* was the last original album released by The Kinks. On 15 June 1996, the band played what was to be their last show – at a festival in Norway, although nobody knew at the time that they wouldn't tour again. Both brothers undertook solo careers whilst other members of the band waited for a phone call which never came, and of course, they went on to other things.

Keyboard player Gordon Edwards passed away on 28 February 2003, and original bassist Pete Quaife died on 23 June 2010. Jim Rodford joined his cousin Rod Argent in The Zombies, and took part in a reunion tour of the band Argent in 2012, but died on 20 January 2018 following a fall at his home. Ian Gibbons also passed away, on 1 August 2019, after playing on many Ray Davies solo projects and tours. John Gosling has – along with most other Kinks band members – performed with the Kast Off Kinks and retired in 2008 (although he has occasionally been persuaded to play again).

John Dalton was one of the founders of the Kast Off Kinks and didn't miss many gigs. However, he was forced to retire from playing in 2021. Andy Pyle went on to play with Wishbone Ash and Gary Moore. He also released a solo album titled *Barrier Language* in 1985. Mark Haley has also remained active and as of 2021, is a member of The Equals. Another still-active ex-Kink is Bob Henrit, who was also a member of the reformed Argent.

Mick Avory has been the main drummer in the Kast Off Kinks, and also formed a 1960s hits band called Class of '64, with Chip Hawkes (The Tremeloes) and Eric Haydock (The Hollies). Mick also replaced Rick Buckler in From The Jam, touring in 2009 with Bruce Foxton.

Dave Davies has continued to tour and record. However, on 30 June 2004, he suffered a stroke whilst in London promoting his album *Bug*. Following physiotherapy, he was able to walk, talk and play guitar again by 2006, thereby restarting his solo career.

Ray Davies has also undertaken a solo career and has gained many awards and plaudits for his songwriting. On 4 January 2004, whilst in New Orleans, he and his girlfriend were victims of a mugging. Ray gave chase and was shot in the leg (Considering Dave had his stroke six months later, 2004 wasn't a great year for the Davies family). On 17 March 2004, Ray was at Buckingham Palace collecting his CBE. In 2012, Ray was given the honour of performing at the closing ceremony of the London Olympic Games as part of a 'Symphony of British Music'. In the 2017 New Year's Honours, Ray was knighted for Services to The Arts.

Rumours have abounded for years that there could at some point be new music from The Kinks – Ray, Dave and Mick have all said that they have been working together. Whether this work will ever be heard, remains to be seen.

We can but hope.

Bibliography and Selected Reading

Clarke, D., (editor)*The Penguin Encyclopedia of Popular Music* (Penguin, 1998)

Davies, D., *Kink* (Boxtree, 1996)

Davies, R., *Waterloo Sunset* (Viking, 1997)

Davies, R., *X-Ray* (The Overlook Press, 2007)

Hinman, D., *All Day And All Of The Night* (Backbeat, 2004)

Jovanovic, R., *God Save The Kinks* (Aurum Press, 2013)

Larkin, C., *Virgin Encyclopedia Of 60s Music* (Virgin, 2002)

Rees, D., Crampton, L., (editors), *Q Encyclopedia Of Rock Stars* (Dorling Kindersley, 1999)

Roberts, D., (editor), *Guinness Book Of British Hit Singles & Albums* (Guinness World Records, 2003)

Rogan, J., *The Complete Guide To The Music Of The Kinks* (Omnibus Press, 1998)

Savage, J., *The Kinks -The Official Biography* (Faber & Faber, 1984)

Tobler, J., *New Musical Express Rock 'n' Roll Years* (Hamlyn, 1992)

White, G.R., *British Hit EPs 1955-1989* (Music Mentor Books, 2014)

Also available from Sonicbond

On Track series

Alan Parsons Project – Steve Swift 978-1-78952-154-2
Tori Amos – Lisa Torem 978-1-78952-142-9
Asia – Peter Braidis 978-1-78952-099-6
Badfinger – Robert Day-Webb 978-1-878952-176-4
Barclay James Harvest – Keith and Monica Domone 978-1-78952-067-5
The Beatles – Andrew Wild 978-1-78952-009-5
The Beatles Solo 1969-1980 – Andrew Wild 978-1-78952-030-9
Blue Oyster Cult – Jacob Holm-Lupo 978-1-78952-007-1
Blur – Matt Bishop 978-178952-164-1
Marc Bolan and T.Rex – Peter Gallagher 978-1-78952-124-5
Kate Bush – Bill Thomas 978-1-78952-097-2
Camel – Hamish Kuzminski 978-1-78952-040-8
Caravan – Andy Boot 978-1-78952-127-6
Cardiacs – Eric Benac 978-1-78952-131-3
Eric Clapton Solo – Andrew Wild 978-1-78952-141-2
The Clash – Nick Assirati 978-1-78952-077-4
Crosby, Stills and Nash – Andrew Wild 978-1-78952-039-2
The Damned – Morgan Brown 978-1-78952-136-8
Deep Purple and Rainbow 1968-79 – Steve Pilkington 978-1-78952-002-6
Dire Straits – Andrew Wild 978-1-78952-044-6
The Doors – Tony Thompson 978-1-78952-137-5
Dream Theater – Jordan Blum 978-1-78952-050-7
Electric Light Orchestra – Barry Delve 978-1-78952-152-8
Elvis Costello and The Attractions – Georg Purvis 978-1-78952-129-0
Emerson Lake and Palmer – Mike Goode 978-1-78952-000-2
Fairport Convention – Kevan Furbank 978-1-78952-051-4
Peter Gabriel – Graeme Scarfe 978-1-78952-138-2
Genesis – Stuart MacFarlane 978-1-78952-005-7
Gentle Giant – Gary Steel 978-1-78952-058-3
Gong – Kevan Furbank 978-1-78952-082-8
Hall and Oates – Ian Abrahams 978-1-78952-167-2
Hawkwind – Duncan Harris 978-1-78952-052-1
Peter Hammill – Richard Rees Jones 978-1-78952-163-4

Roy Harper – Opher Goodwin 978-1-78952-130-6
Jimi Hendrix – Emma Stott 978-1-78952-175-7
The Hollies – Andrew Darlington 978-1-78952-159-7
Iron Maiden – Steve Pilkington 978-1-78952-061-3
Jefferson Airplane – Richard Butterworth 978-1-78952-143-6
Jethro Tull – Jordan Blum 978-1-78952-016-3
Elton John in the 1970s – Peter Kearns 978-1-78952-034-7
The Incredible String Band – Tim Moon 978-1-78952-107-8
Iron Maiden – Steve Pilkington 978-1-78952-061-3
Judas Priest – John Tucker 978-1-78952-018-7
Kansas – Kevin Cummings 978-1-78952-057-6
The Kinks – Martin Hutchinson 978-1-78952-172-6
Korn – Matt Karpe 978-1-78952-153-5
Led Zeppelin – Steve Pilkington 978-1-78952-151-1
Level 42 – Matt Philips 978-1-78952-102-3
Little Feat – 978-1-78952-168-9
Aimee Mann – Jez Rowden 978-1-78952-036-1
Joni Mitchell – Peter Kearns 978-1-78952-081-1
The Moody Blues – Geoffrey Feakes 978-1-78952-042-2
Motorhead – Duncan Harris 978-1-78952-173-3
Mike Oldfield – Ryan Yard 978-1-78952-060-6
Opeth – Jordan Blum 978-1-78-952-166-5
Tom Petty – Richard James 978-1-78952-128-3
Porcupine Tree – Nick Holmes 978-1-78952-144-3
Queen – Andrew Wild 978-1-78952-003-3
Radiohead – William Allen 978-1-78952-149-8
Renaissance – David Detmer 978-1-78952-062-0
The Rolling Stones 1963-80 – Steve Pilkington 978-1-78952-017-0
The Smiths and Morrissey – Tommy Gunnarsson 978-1-78952-140-5
Status Quo the Frantic Four Years – Richard James 978-1-78952-160-3
Steely Dan – Jez Rowden 978-1-78952-043-9
Steve Hackett – Geoffrey Feakes 978-1-78952-098-9
Thin Lizzy – Graeme Stroud 978-1-78952-064-4
Toto – Jacob Holm-Lupo 978-1-78952-019-4
U2 – Eoghan Lyng 978-1-78952-078-1
UFO – Richard James 978-1-78952-073-6
The Who – Geoffrey Feakes 978-1-78952-076-7
Roy Wood and the Move – James R Turner

978-1-78952-008-8
Van Der Graaf Generator – Dan Coffey
978-1-78952-031-6
Yes – Stephen Lambe 978-1-78952-001-9
Frank Zappa 1966 to 1979 – Eric Benac
978-1-78952-033-0
Warren Zevon – Peter Gallagher
978-1-78952-170-2
10CC – Peter Kearns 978-1-78952-054-5

Decades Series
The Bee Gees in the 1960s –
Andrew Mon Hughes et al 978-1-78952-148-1
The Bee Gees in the 1970s –
Andrew Mon Hughes et al 978-1-78952-179-5
Black Sabbath in the 1970s – Chris Sutton
978-1-78952-171-9
Britpop – Peter Richard Adams and Matt Pooler
978-1-78952-169-6
Alice Cooper in the 1970s – Chris Sutton
978-1-78952-104-7
Curved Air in the 1970s – Laura Shenton
978-1-78952-069-9
Bob Dylan in the 1980s – Don Klees
978-1-78952-157-3
Fleetwood Mac in the 1970s – Andrew Wild 978-1-78952-105-4
Focus in the 1970s – Stephen Lambe
978-1-78952-079-8
Free and Bad Company in the 1970s –
John Van der Kiste 978-1-78952-178-8
Genesis in the 1970s – Bill Thomas
978178952-146-7
George Harrison in the 1970s – Eoghan Lyng 978-1-78952-174-0
Marillion in the 1980s – Nathaniel Webb
978-1-78952-065-1
Mott the Hoople and Ian Hunter in the 1970s –
John Van der Kiste 978-1-78-952-162-7
Pink Floyd In The 1970s – Georg Purvis
978-1-78952-072-9
Tangerine Dream in the 1970s –
Stephen Palmer 978-1-78952-161-0
The Sweet in the 1970s – Darren Johnson
978-1-78952-139-9
Uriah Heep in the 1970s – Steve Pilkington
978-1-78952-103-0
Yes in the 1980s – Stephen Lambe with David
Watkinson 978-1-78952-125-2

On Screen series
Carry On… – Stephen Lambe
978-1-78952-004-0
David Cronenberg – Patrick Chapman
978-1-78952-071-2

Doctor Who: The David Tennant Years –
Jamie Hailstone 978-1-78952-066-8
James Bond – Andrew Wild –
978-1-78952-010-1
Monty Python – Steve Pilkington
978-1-78952-047-7
Seinfeld Seasons 1 to 5 – Stephen Lambe
978-1-78952-012-5

Other Books
1967: A Year In Psychedelic Rock
978-1-78952-155-9
1970: A Year In Rock – John Van der Kiste
978-1-78952-147-4
1973: The Golden Year of Progressive Rock
978-1-78952-165-8
Babysitting A Band On The Rocks –
G.D. Praetorius 978-1-78952-106-1
Eric Clapton Sessions – Andrew Wild
978-1-78952-177-1
Derek Taylor: For Your Radioactive Children –
Andrew Darlington 978-1-78952-038-5
The Golden Road: The Recording History of The
Grateful Dead –
John Kilbride 978-1-78952-156-6
Iggy and The Stooges On Stage 1967-1974 –
Per Nilsen 978-1-78952-101-6
Jon Anderson and the Warriors – the road to Yes –
David Watkinson 978-1-78952-059-0
Nu Metal: A Definitive Guide – Matt Karpe
978-1-78952-063-7
Tommy Bolin: In and Out of Deep Purple – Laura
Shenton 978-1-78952-070-5
Maximum Darkness – Deke Leonard
978-1-78952-048-4
Maybe I Should've Stayed In Bed –
Deke Leonard 978-1-78952-053-8
Psychedelic Rock in 1967 – Kevan Furbank
978-1-78952-155-9
The Twang Dynasty – Deke Leonard
978-1-78952-049-1

and many more to come!

Would you like to write for Sonicbond Publishing?
We are mainly a music publisher, but we also occasionally
publish in other genres including film and television. At Sonicbond
Publishing we are always on the look-out for authors, particularly for
our two main series, On Track and Decades.

Mixing fact with in depth analysis, the On Track series examines
the entire recorded work of a particular musical artist or group. All
genres are considered from easy listening and jazz to 60s soul to 90s
pop, via rock and metal.

The Decades series singles out a particular decade in an artist or
group's history and focuses on that decade in more detail than may
be allowed in the On Track series.

While professional writing experience would, of course, be
an advantage, the most important qualification is to have real
enthusiasm and knowledge of your subject. First-time authors are
welcomed, but the ability to write well in English is essential.

Sonicbond Publishing has distribution throughout Europe and
North America, and all our books are also published in E-book form.
Authors will be paid a royalty based on sales of their book.
Further details about our books are available from
www.sonicbondpublishing.com. To contact us, complete the
contact form there or email info@sonicbondpublishing.co.uk